Acclaim for Grace Street: A Sister's Memoir of Grief & Gratitude

Maureen Callahan Smith writes with courage and honesty about the heart-breaking journey she walked with her sister Kathy through her sister's cancer and ultimate death. This memoir is of inestimable value for family, community, and caregivers.

Smith says, "We cannot know as something is happening what meaning it will hold for our lives." Yet as she reaches back and describes those days, she offers not only the raw demands and great challenges a family faces, but also the beauty of loving. Her moving description of the vast quiet and power that followed Kathy's last breath allows you to enter the room yourself. She concludes that "every moment [in life] is urgent and precious." Surely a message for all times.

—Paula D'Arcy, author of *Stars at Night* and *Winter of the Heart*

D1240040

This jewel of book will touch you, and it will change you. It reveals the gift that is available to all of us in our deepest loves and losses. This story of two sisters' undying love invites us to walk through this precious life holding gratitude in one hand and grief in the other. It is the owning and honoring of both that makes our lives matter, makes them mean something, and makes them more beautiful.

Thank you, Maureen Callahan Smith, for reminding us that we are made for exactly this. Showing up fully, sharing the human journey wholeheartedly with the people that we love most in the world, is not only the gift of being alive, it's our true reason for being here. This story makes me want to be more brave, to show up more fully, and to let love, not fear, lead.

—Sue Cross, Founder of Living the Possible – Creative Engagement Coaching for People Living with Alzheimer's

Maureen Callahan Smith

(Author photo by Michael Rodman.)

Author and clinical social worker Maureen Callahan Smith, LICSW, has a private practice on the North Shore of Boston specializing in trauma work and helping people navigate grief and loss. In her work she draws on decades of meditation, yoga, and writing practice. She lives with her husband Tony in the greater Boston area.

Some names and identifying details have been changed to protect the privacy of individuals. I have tried to recreate events, locales and conversations from my memories, and from contemporaneous journals.

This book is not intended as a substitute for the medical advice of physicians. The descriptions of cancer treatments and bone marrow transplant (BMT) reflect the state of treatment at the time.

Although we have made every effort to ensure that the information in this book was correct at press time, the author and publisher do not assume and hereby disclaim any liability to any party for any loss, damage, or disruption caused by errors or omissions, whether such errors or omissions result from negligence, accident, or any other cause.

All poems by Maureen Callahan Smith. Excerpt from *Life Prayers*, by James Bertilino, reprinted on p. 107 with the author's permission. Author photo by Michael Rodman; photos on pp. 297, 300 by Jenna Medina. All other photos are from the author's family collection, including pp. 297 and 300 and the cover photo, all taken by her father, Colbert Smith.

ISBN: 978-1-953253-00-2
Gray Dove Press
www.graydovepress.com
Editor: Patricia Crotty
Cover photo: Maureen and Kathy, 1954, by Colbert Smith
Cover and Book Design: Harvey Shepard

Grace Street

A Sister's Memoir of
Grief & Gratitude

Maureen Callahan Smith

Gray Dove Press

On earth,
it goes like this:
our most golden, precious moments must come
to letting go

and

more stunning than the sun in its most dazzling farewell
Are these shining human hearts, which,
knowing this,

go on loving anyway.

—from *Wingaersheek*, August, 2003

Forward

I wrote this story because I needed to, when, so many years after losing my sister, I found myself daily, hourly sometimes, still being touched by life in some way that brought up her "missing-ness." Like an invisible shard in my heart, it doesn't show when you look at me, but there it sits in the center of my chest, a shard now turned to crystal that casts its light and color over my life. Inside that crystal, Kathy is still with me. I know I am not alone in this experience.

We are so afraid of death in our culture, and we have such trouble talking about it, despite the obvious reality that the experience of losing someone we adore is "baked into" our very existence. My generation, the "Woodstock" generation, is now busy learning about home care and hospice, living wills and natural burials.

Every death is different. Every family is different. This is just one story. It was written in the belief that the more we share our stories, the greater the chance we have of shedding our odd shame about illness, and our silence about grief. That as much as we desperately wish to avoid the pain, even agony of loss, we are meant, as Ram Dass wrote, to be "Walking Each Other Home." That in fact, we have hearts made for this.

Dedication

To all the devoted caregivers, medical professionals, and patients striving to live.

To my sister Kathy's husband, an Olympian in the devotion department.

To her wonderful sons, who absorbed everything they've been through and turned it into more love (and laughter, and music).

To my husband Anthony, whose unwavering love for me, for our family, and for Kathy, even through the darkest of times, is the treasure of my life. Writing this book has taken years made up of many, many hours and weekends. For your love and patience, meals and laughter, readings and never-wavering encouragement, I am profoundly thankful.

And to my sister Kathy, whose devotion set the bar. The best parts of me are because of you. I carry you with me every day.

Ireland

Inis Mór, County Galway, Ireland

The gray stone walls of Inis Mór, County Galway.

I am standing in the bustling pub of a small hotel on Inis Mór, the largest of the Aran Islands off the west coast of Ireland. The stone facade of the hotel is built from the gray stones that cover the island, hundreds of thousands of them forming a lacey gridwork of walls. The hotel sits about fifty steps from the edge of the sea, on Kilronan Harbor.

It is a family wedding day. Fifty of us flew out from Boston four days ago, and we have just danced into the reception to the joyous music of "I Gotta Feeling," by The Black Eyed

Peas. After the brilliant landscape of sea and sky and radiant green land, the pub room feels like nighttime. Dark paneling covers the walls, setting off sparkling rows of amber-hued bottles beckoning travelers to the bar.

The party is well underway, and I am locked in conversation when I hear the voice of Patrick, the groom, over the sound system. He is my sister's eldest, my nephew and godson.

"Mimi?" Patrick calls out. "Where's Mimi?" he repeats, using the family nickname he gave me as a toddler, when he couldn't say Maureen. He is standing in the middle of the room and scanning the crowd, microphone in hand.

Startled, I turn and he catches my eye and smiles. Bridegroom jacket already tossed to the corner, he stands in his fancy wedding shirt, tie loosened and sleeves rolled up, ready to celebrate. His frame is tall and lanky like my Dad's, his dark curls, cropped close for the occasion, and black-framed glasses give him the look of a slightly serious hipster, belying his irreverent sense of humor. He opens his arms, watching me approach.

"Mimi?" he calls again, gesturing now toward the empty dance floor.

Tears spring. I swallow hard as I move toward him. The room is hushed as the music begins. My heart shakes as we step to the center of the dance floor. It is the mother's dance.

Fall, 1993

Ordinary Magic

The two couples, autumn in the Berkshires, 1993.

I keep a photo over my kitchen sink of my sister Kathy and me, with our partners behind us. Kathy is smiling at the camera on this bright fall day, her petite frame bundled up in a lavender turtleneck and blue fleece jacket. Dark, chin-length waves frame a delicate face and smiling dark eyes. She looks pretty and happy and well.

The photo was taken on the golden autumn weekend when I brought my new sweetheart Tony home to meet her for the first time. There was a long-standing tradition in our family of sisters interfering on behalf of romance. My parents were literally the boy-and-girl next door, and their marriage was partially engineered by Mom's younger sister, Alice. The story goes that my Dad seemed quite content to continue courting my mom while living next door. My aunt, it was said, took him by the arm and walked him downtown one day to the window of Jolly Jewelers, directed him to the engagement rings in the window, and gave him a healthy poke in the ribs. In his own defense, my Dad would point out, he was not stupid. He took the hint and he and my mother were married later that same year, in June of 1946, soon after the war ended.

So, Kathy's approval was important to me, but any nervousness we might have felt swiftly evaporated as she welcomed Tony in her warm, engaging way. She had settled in the small town where we grew up, North Adams, a former manufacturing and railroad center nestled in the hills of northwestern Massachusetts. On this weekend, the Berkshires were at their most glorious, with the strong bone-warming light and azure blue sky that only comes in October, the air scented with sunshine, the ground a patchwork of fallen leaves in hues of pomegranate and mustard.

"So, Maureen says you grew up in Pittsfield, of all places! How funny is that?!" Kathy said. "You grew up half an hour away from us, and the two of you never met 'til you were both living in Boston!" They talked about people they knew in common and then found even more shared ground discussing where the Red Sox had landed by the season's end. Kathy was a fierce and knowledgeable sports fan. Her two passions were the Boston Red Sox and the Duke basketball team, and in her home, major league baseball and college basketball's March Madness were sacred seasons. From her faithful post by the TV, she would fill the living room with hoots of enthusiasm, one-sided arguments with the refs, and informed play-by-play for her companions.

At one point, long before Tony came into my life, Kathy's inner sports fan and her inner matchmaker teamed up and hatched a plan to liven up my love life. I'd been single for several years after a difficult divorce, and she became especially interested in figuring out some way to get me introduced to Red Sox pitching ace Dennis Eckersley. It quickly became clear that she had given her latest project some thought.

"I think he's really a nice guy. And he's certainly cute. I think he'd be perfect for you," she said, her eyes sparkling, no doubt at the thought of Dennis Eckersley becoming a permanent fixture at Thanksgiving dinner.

"Kathy!" I laughed. "On what planet does that make sense? I don't know a damn thing about baseball. You're the one who should meet him!"

"Well, I'm taken. But don't rule it out. You know, opposites can attract. And you could learn, couldn't you? I'm sure he'd be glad to teach you."

I shook my head while she rattled off possible ways I might meet "Eck." The thing was, she was half serious. She knew I was ready to meet someone, and I loved her—among so many other reasons—for her whole-hearted optimism that, whether or not it was "Eck," I would meet the right someone.

Then I met Tony. Ten years after my first marriage ended, I was set up on a blind date with him through his sister, Rosie. Both Berkshire County girls transplanted to Boston, she and I met as social workers in the psychiatry department at a local community hospital. As we became good friends, she would eye me periodically and ask, "So, are you seeing anyone these days? I think I have a brother for you!"

As luck would have it, each time it came up, Tony or I was involved with someone else. But Rosie persisted, and finally one day it seemed that the stars were aligned.

Our first date in early December 1992 was a beauty. I opened the door to find a runner-thin man in a rumpled khaki jacket. At six foot four, he towered over me. His collar was turned up and his face, framed by a silvering beard and thick, graying hair, was beautiful, soft and kind, with tender blue eyes. We drove through snow flurries to a white clapboard church lit with candles and decked with winter greens to hear a Maine folk trio sing sea shanties and Christmas carols. We sat beside each other that first evening, both of us, we later confided, quietly filled with a sweet sense of possibility.

Our next date fell a week before Christmas. Neither of us was sure how to handle the question of a holiday gift. We'd scarcely known each other two weeks. When it came time to say goodnight, Tony shyly reached for a small gift-wrapped package and handed it to me, murmuring, "Just a little something to wish you a happy Christmas." At the same time, I had reached into my bag to offer him a similarly sized package. We opened them and laughed with nervous amazement. We had given each other the same book: *Ordinary Magic, Everyday Life as Spiritual Path*, by John Welwood. While we had been pleased to discover that we shared an interest in meditation and yoga, and indeed, that's partly what had led Rosie to play matchmaker, we were slightly dumbstruck by the synchronicity of the Christmas packages. Over the next few months, love bloomed, more precious and appreciated at mid-life. Ordinary magic, indeed.

Now I had brought my new love home, eager to share him with everyone and to get my sister's blessing. We spent a happy weekend with Kathy, her husband Greg and their sons Patrick and Liam (ages 14 and 11) finding out, as I'd known all along, that Tony fit in as if he had always been there. His was a large, close family and with all the ribbing that went on among his siblings, his goofball sense of humor was finely honed. Comfortable and happy around kids, he moved in right away to engage the boys. He struggled a bit to make a connection with Liam, who was a bit quiet and slow to warm up to him.

"So, are you reading anything good these days?" Tony tried.

Liam shrugged, "I'm reading a book about a magician, Harry Houdini."

"Harry Houdini!" Tony said, "Are you kidding? He's one of my favorites! I've read all about him too!"

And shortly Liam was parked beside Tony on the family sofa, the two of them pouring over his Houdini book. Next thing we knew, Tony was offering to tie him up to see if he could escape. Liam was in heaven and spent a happy half-hour huffing and grimacing as he wriggled proudly out of Tony's increasingly complicated knots.

Early in the evening, Kathy summoned me for a confab. "Let me see you in my office," she whispered, nodding toward the kitchen where we could have a private word.

"HE is a KEEPER!" she told me. "Hands down. Best Boy-friend Ever, no contest. What a great guy. Do NOT screw this up!" she laughed, grabbing my shoulders, and pulling me close for a hug.

Prom Night

It all began on the most beautiful of May evenings. I was at home in Arlington, a suburb close to Boston that borders the city of Cambridge. Living together by then, Tony and I shared a large first-floor apartment, and with the wide, waist-level windows of our kitchen flung open, I looked out into trees alight with buds and a back yard glowing in the low-slung sun. The air was washed by recent days of rain and scented by plants large and small, throwing up new growth so abundantly that you could practically hear it happening. It was a late afternoon brimming with springtime well-being and promise.

I was working on an art project on the kitchen counter, trying out a new way of creating photo transfers from slides. I had learned about the technique through my recent membership at Turtle Studios, a cooperative artists' studio in nearby Watertown. As a clinical social worker, I had recently taken a new job at a private agency doing in-home support for teens in long-term foster care and their families. It was work that I found both rewarding and stressful, sometimes in the extreme. By joining the art studio, I'd stepped into a different world, one where I felt both excited and self-conscious about all there was to learn.

As I was engrossed in my project, the phone rang. It was my 79-year-old mother, calling from her home in western Massachusetts. Mom lived alone in a senior housing center, which had been built in the old school building where Kathy and I had gone to school through the twelfth grade. She had been living there for several years, since my Dad's vascular dementia had required him to be admitted to a small nursing care facility in nearby Williamstown. Her phone call was not unusual, since we often spoke daily. As I cradled the phone under my chin, I held the transferred image up to the light.

As soon I heard the tone of my mother's voice, I dropped the photo to the counter. "I think you need to come out here, honey, pretty quick," she said. "Kathy went in to see Dr. Finley today, and he's put her in the hospital. She's at Berkshire Medical." I was having a hard time following. I'd just talked with Kathy the evening before, and she'd seemed fine. She told me she was going to see her doctor, but there was nothing worrisome about it. We were both pretty good about our annual check-ups.

"Wait, Mom, what do you mean? For what? She hasn't been sick ..."

"Her blood work." My mother cut to the chase. "He took some blood tests, and her numbers are way off. She was out to lunch with the girls at the River House in Williamstown, and Dr. Finley called to tell Greg to get her and bring her to the ER right away."

That was the beginning.

I hung up the phone, threw a few things in a bag and leapt into my car to drive the two and a half hours to Berkshire Medical Center (BMC) in Pittsfield. I found Kathy's husband Greg and my mother, known to all as Millie, sitting beside

Kathy's bed in a tableau that would soon become familiar. Petite, white-haired, and with an indomitable core of equal parts will power and faith, Mom, in deference to her age, occupied the one comfortable chair in the room. She was dressed in her Mom uniform: drapey floral blouse, matching pastel slacks, and spotless white walking shoes that she replaced every year, whether she needed to or not.

Greg—graying, wire-spectacled, and worried—sat close to Kathy, who was prone in her hospital bed, and suddenly looked shockingly pale and thin. The sight of her, the sense of urgency with which she'd been admitted, and the stunningly low numbers from her blood work sent a chill through the normal, sunny spring evening. I had to steel myself as I approached her, breathing deeply to keep my fear at bay.

Somber but not cowed, Kathy gave me a wry look when she saw me. "Well, what do you think? This could really suck, couldn't it?" Then she immediately turned the conversation to me. "How was the traffic on the Pike coming out? Was it bad?"

"Don't worry sweetie," I reassured her. "Whatever this is, we got it. Whatever it takes. You're going to be fine." Unaware of all that lay ahead, I was convinced that we could will her recovery with sheer love and good teamwork.

That evening, as a colorful sunset streamed through the slatted hospital blinds, we met with an oncologist and were given a diagnosis: non-Hodgkin's lymphoma (NHL), not yet analyzed for cell type or stage.

We were stunned. None of us had seen this coming. There had been no worrisome lump, no days of waiting.

Only five hours ago, Kathy was at lunch with her girlfriends and all was still as it should be in our world. As Dr. Spector spoke, he looked out at three faces that were slack with shock and nearly as pale as Kathy's. And still. The room was still, as if some force had stolen our capacity to react. The most we seemed capable of was staring at his face as we each scrambled within ourselves to absorb what we were being told. Hoping that, like a Times Square headline ticker, he would deliver better news if we only watched long enough.

At first, those words "non-Hodgkin's lymphoma" didn't quite register. I had vaguely heard of it before and thought it was some unusual form of cancer, maybe not "real" cancer. Probably quite treatable. What did that "non" refer to, after all? But propped against the oversized pillows in her hospital bed, Kathy looked so small and serious, her mouth a tense line across her face, her dark eyes darting from us to the doctor and back, her banter silenced. It was the gravity of her face that shook me finally, introducing a worm of fear into my gut that, after that evening, never really left.

I looked over at my mother. In her working years as head nurse of a busy medical-surgical floor, she was never one to be intimidated by doctors. Instead, I had witnessed her in firm command of her ward while green young doctors followed her brisk pace like nervous pups. She would normally have been full of questions at a time like this, but she too was muted by the news, her face a mask of puzzled fear.

The oncologist Dr. Spector was a compact, silver-haired man who managed to radiate warmth and equanimity even as he delivered the hard news. From the outset, his tone was matter-of-fact yet upbeat. A stranger that night, he would become a confidante whom Kathy came to trust deeply.

He stood with us in the close hospital room and offered a brief primer on non-Hodgkin's lymphoma. We learned that NHL is a cancer of the lymphatic system, which is part of the immune system, and that there are many forms of NHL. We would need to wait for test results to learn which type Kathy had and how advanced the disease was. I had a sense that Dr. Spector recognized the state we were in and was pacing the news somewhat, particularly in the presence of my mom. Only in hindsight would I recall that there seemed to be a disconnect between his matter-of-fact demeanor and a new somberness in my sister, as if he had either shared more frankly with her in private, or she'd sensed something more ominous in how badly she'd felt.

As we talked more that evening, it came out that she'd been feeling poorly indeed: fatigue, shortness of breath, and night sweats, all of which she'd attributed to menopause. And she'd lost weight, gradually but significantly, from a frame that was 5′4″ and delicate to begin with. As we took in the news, we were all asking ourselves how we hadn't noticed how thin she had gotten. But the shortness of breath was the most worrisome symptom. We learned that recently she'd had to pause to rest when climbing the single flight of stairs at home. That didn't jibe with menopause and was part of the reason she'd made the appointment with her doctor in the first place.

As I looked back on the initial diagnosis, when the whole world seemed slightly tilted off its axis, I realized that in the physical exam, Dr. Spector had probably been able to feel the telling signs of advanced disease in the enlarged lymph nodes and spleen in Kathy's abdomen, an ominous contributor to her shortness of breath.

In the meantime, transfusions were in order to restore the level of her blood platelets and fortify her missing-in-action immune system. She required four units over the next day or two. But it was prom weekend, and whatever the doctor's agenda, Kathy had her own, and it had nothing to do with her platelets. However slightly built and winsome her appearance, Kathy would prove from the start that our mother's gritty mettle had not skipped a generation, especially where it intersected with the well-being of anyone she loved. In her relationships, she was a warrior of loyalty. It was one of the defining threads of her character. So, once those new platelets began to take hold overnight and restore some color to her cheeks, her "Irish," as Mom called her feistiness, began to make its presence felt.

Just after dawn the next day, Greg and I slipped into her room, as we both wanted to hear what the doctors proposed to do next. We learned fast that the only way to get actual face-time with the physicians was to rise early and catch them during their close-to-dawn visits. Kathy was already awake when we arrived, and she prepared to face down the battalion of coffee-toting residents accompanying Dr. Spector on his 6 a.m. rounds as if girding for battle. She washed her face, brushed her teeth and hair, donned her own robe over the hospital-issued johnnie, and pulled herself upright, ready for her next move. When the phalanx of MDs gathered at her bedside to discuss her treatment options, she made it clear that she was having none of it until they assured her that she would be sprung in time to see Patrick off for his prom night.

"I am not missing my son's dance," she began, once initial good mornings were dispensed with. "I'm sorry, but I'm just not. You're gonna have to figure something out, because tomorrow night, come hell or high water, I'm going to be on my front porch taking pictures with my son." She frowned as she finished, as if to intercept all incoming arguments.

The next morning, her blood work was still marginal enough that the crowd of "white coats," as she had begun calling them, came bearing a compromise as if it were an olive branch. She would be allowed to go home for a few hours on a pass—just enough time to help Patrick get ready, take some photos and see him and his date off—and then return to the hospital for more monitoring and transfusing. She accepted their offer and leaned back against her pillows, satisfied.

Life in the Infusion Room

The next day provided a bit of sorely needed uplift. The hospital team initiated some treatment steps to help Kathy begin regaining strength. The first stop was the infusion room and more platelets, to supplement Kathy's decimated supply. As the nurse hung the platelet bag at her side, Kathy rolled her eyes in mock horror. "Don't tell me that's my lunch. I can still eat, can't I?!"

Reassuring her that yes of course, they were very interested in her eating, the young nurse offered some typical hospital fare. Tuna salad on white? Chicken salad? Vanilla pudding? Graham crackers?

"It all sounds just ducky, but from now on, I think I'll be ordering take-out from the Highland," Kathy told her, referring to a favorite eatery around the corner. "It's probably illegal to sneak in a beer though, huh?"

With reclining chairs and IV poles on wheels that rolled around the room at the touch of a finger, the infusion room occupied a beige hospital space that felt like a basement. As we settled into those first few transfusions, we began to fall into the division of labor that would carry us through the next many months. When he could, Greg stayed glued to Kathy's side. When the boys or his work called, I would take over.

Greg and I had known each other since we were teens. In fact, I had fixed Kathy up with him for their first date—that sister thing again—and when they got engaged, I rolled five yards of ivory crepe down my front hall to cut and sew her wedding dress. He was like a brother to me, so sharing duties came easily.

"So how about that chicken salad while we watch a movie?" Kathy asked. She gestured to a pile of DVDs on the nearby table. "They have 'Four Weddings and a Funeral.' I know we've seen it, but let's watch it again, it's got Hugh Grant," she smiled at me.

We left the funeral reference right there, untouched. In this moment, I took Kathy's lead, as we all would throughout the journey. Whatever she wanted or needed to get through the fear, the boredom, the anxious waiting, that's what we were all about. Plus, well, you know. Hugh Grant.

From the start, we looked for any chances to keep things as close as possible to what Kathy referred to as "regular life." Two sisters eating chicken salad on white and watching "Four Weddings and a Funeral" together. What could be more normal? Except that we were sitting in a hospital room full of beeps and clicks, and my sister was tethered to a large plastic bag while the life-saving liquids it held dripped into her arm.

The nurse stopped in again to check on the platelet flow. She commented on the lovely clothes and the fascinating array of hats that were on display in the film. Kathy watched as the nurse adjusted her IV. As usual, her mind was busy with other matters, and she turned back to me, already chuckling at what she was about to say.

"Oh! Did I tell you? I don't think I did—this week, I had a revelation! I think I've discovered the secret to life!"

"Really?!" I asked, happy to play straight man. "Do tell!"

"Matching undies!" she proclaimed. She proceeded to regale her amused nurse and myself with the story of a recent sale at Macy's and her splurge to buy three matching sets of undergarments. "In lilac, yellow, and black. Because you always need black. And I'm telling you right now, it does wonders to start off your day all matched up in nice new undies. You feel like the Queen of Sheba! I'm not kidding! You should try it!" she said, finishing the last bite of her sandwich.

The nurse lowered the lights as she exited, so we could watch the film. Just moments later, I glanced over to see that Kathy had drifted off. When the nurse returned a half hour later to check on the IV, she bent to whisper something to me.

"She has such a great family. You are all going to be really important in helping her with this. It's wonderful that you two are friends as well as sisters. You don't always see that. You two are lucky," she said.

As Kathy dozed, I thought about the nurse's comment, and another movie began to play inside my head of the many times in my life when Kathy had been there for me. It took me back to the 1980s and the time leading up to the breakup of my first marriage. I had been working at a community mental health center, co-directing an early intervention program for at-risk infants and toddlers and their families.

The separation and divorce after a 10-year marriage had been painful in the extreme. It had followed the death of our first born, Megan, who was born six weeks prematurely and lived only three days. After a carefree and glowing pregnancy, the loss was crushing and was followed by two earlier-term miscarriages. A series of tests revealed structural problems related to a hormone my mom had been prescribed early in her pregnancy with me, after she herself had suffered two miscarriages.

DES, a synthetic estrogen, was touted at the time as a treatment to prevent further pregnancy loss. Yet it would prove not only ineffective in preventing miscarriage, but also disastrous for the developing reproductive tracts of many children born to mothers who took it. The pharmaceutical company continued to market the drug for decades after they had evidence—which they concealed—of its potential for harm. The upshot was that my ability to carry a child to term was put at risk before I was even born, in ways that would become apparent only many years later. Surgical attempts at repair of the structural issues were followed by further complications, and then further surgeries. The decade of my twenties passed in a blur of hospital rooms and grief.

During all of it, Kathy was at my side, my companion and whatever-it-takes supporter. She witnessed it all. As I sat at Megan's bassinette in the neo-natal nursery holding her tiny fingers and willing her strength, I looked up to see Kathy's worried face, watching us in the window. Later, as we struggled with mourning my first child and waiting for another that never came, she would glance at me across some family event full of the adorable babies who were appearing on the scene, with a look that said, "Uh-huh. I see you. I know." Or she'd come up behind me, throw an arm over my shoulders, pull me close and stay there for a bit. Again and again, our connection made the unbearable more bearable.

Side by side had always been our way of life. "Irish twins" separated by just thirteen months, we shared everything from matching plaid flannel shirts to a room with maple poster beds and gaudy fifties wallpaper. Photo albums from my Dad's Argus camera days are filled with Kathy and Maureen pictures: as toddlers in footie pajamas having tea parties by the Christmas tree, as little girls playing Mary and Joseph in robes rigged up from chenille bedspreads, and as long-haired teens hunched shoulder-to-shoulder before Kathy's shrine to Carl Yastrzemski, Jim Lonborg, and the 1967 Red Sox.

Our relationship was one lifelong conversation, a great running gab that covered the delirium of Beatlemania (hers was Paul, mine Ringo), saw one another through the Parade of Wrong Boyfriends, survived the family dramas, and joked, but not really, about winding up knitting in the nursing home together. When we discussed this particular chapter of our future she would eye me and joke, "But one of us is gonna have to learn to knit pretty soon, don't you think?"

Our sisterhood felt more like sibling synergy than sibling rivalry. Together, we were better, happier, and braver than we were alone. I reflected back to her the accomplished mother, wife, and parenting coach she had become. And she held firm to hope when my own way into that world of marriage and mothering seemed to have been lost.

I was grateful for so many reasons to have her at my side through those difficult years, but I was not surprised. When

Kathy & Maureen, 1953 (photos from Dad's Argus camera).

Kathy & Maureen, 1953.

Maureen & Kathy, 1953.

Kathy & Maureen, Christmas, 1955.

we were little, our dad was hospitalized for over a year with a relapse of the tuberculosis that he'd suffered from during his college years at Holy Cross. With the loss of his health and livelihood, he struggled with depression. So early on, Kathy and I learned to lean in when things got rough, our every impulse aimed at helping one another. Later, during the darkest chapter of my life, I felt blessed to have her with me, offering her irreplaceable mix of fierce concern, thoughtful tracking of the details, and keen sense of when to soothe things with her dry humor or a molasses cookie and a cup of hot tea.

But the losses took their toll, including eventually the end of my marriage. Before I knew it, I found myself sleeping on Kathy and Greg's sofa while I tried to figure out which of the slippery rocks in front of me to set my foot on next. With the help of therapy and time, the fog of the divorce began to lift and a sense of new direction emerged. With the combination of excitement and trepidation that accompanies new adventures, I decided to move to Boston to pursue a master's degree in clinical social work.

The move presented a challenge for Kathy and me. She and Greg had lived in Houston for two years before moving back to North Adams when she was pregnant with Patrick, and I had missed her keenly during that time. We'd gotten used to being in and out of each other's kitchens whenever we wished and knew it would be a huge change to live hours apart again. Mom was having her own difficulty with my divorce, and my upcoming move. But Boston was closer than Houston, and Kathy and Greg never wavered from some version of "You go, girl!" We adopted the attitude that my new home was just a three-hour road trip away and held great possibilities for family visits. In turn, I treasured my visits home, where I discovered I could appreciate the beauty of the Berkshires with fresh eyes.

It was not uncommon, during those first months of my living in Boston, for me to return "home" for weekend visits. And, as Kathy and I went about errands around town, as often as not, I would find my eyes wandering up to the undulating horizon, the town's skyline encircled by hills and forest. "Wow, it is *so* beautiful here!" I would find myself muttering, at which point Kathy would nudge me in the ribs and reply with an eye roll, laughing, "Oh, please!"

One of those weekend visits home found Kathy and me sitting in her living room with tea in hand and Kathy's cat curled up at her feet.

"Why don't you stay for dinner," she asked. "You're getting too skinny. We're grilling some burgers and Patrick and Liam would love some auntie time. How can you resist us?" I never could, and wasn't about to start then, happy to prolong our visit.

She was sitting in the Queen-Anne-style chair that I had bequeathed to her after my divorce, its cinnamon color the sole bright spark among the restful taupes of her living room. At that point, I was in a phase well-known to friends and family of divorcing parties, where I could not stop talking about it. And while I was living with raw uncertainty about my life, she somehow knew before I did that I would survive, demonstrating her faith in an offer that I never saw coming.

After delivering the latest installment of the Awfulness, we had moved on to chatting about mundane matters: our hair, whether or not she should stencil her front porch, and the preschool adventures of Patrick, her eldest.

At some point, Kathy shifted and fixed me with the intent look she would get when she had something to say, her forehead furrowed, lips pursed. "You know," she said, "this *is* all going to get better. You're in the worst of it right now, but we Irish girls don't go down without a fight. You're gonna be fine."

I told her for the hundredth time that I didn't know how I would have survived the past few years without her—and Greg's—unconditional love. The unconditional part was important, as things were still rocky with those in my world who were flummoxed by the marital split, and foremost in the ranks of the flummoxed was my very Catholic mom.

"Well, we both know you're landing on your feet from this. And, I have something I want to tell you. Something I want you to think about. Greg and I have talked and—when you're ready, one day, if you want—I could carry a baby for you."

I was seated on the sofa, right beside her, and for a few seconds I couldn't breathe. "You ... *what*?" I managed. "You, you ... what? Are you serious?"

Erect in the high-backed chair, she locked onto my eyes and her unblinking gaze answered my question. She was utterly serious. While surrogate pregnancy has become more common in recent years, in 1985 this was a startling offer. As I tried to digest her words, a knot of emotion formed in my throat.

"Oh my God, Kath. I don't know what to say. That is the most amazing thing anyone has ..."

"Like I said," she broke in, buying me time to collect myself, "not right now. But it won't be long before you'll be finished with grad school and working, and you could do it. We'd help. All your friends would help. You'd be such an amazing mother."

I reached over and pulled her to me, overcome and shaking. I'd worked from age thirteen, saving money. I'd done well in school, then married, bought a practical two-family home, then began trying to start a family. Everything by the book. Yet, despite my valiant attempts, the longed-for goal of becoming a mother had remained out of reach. Was it possible that it could still happen? I asked her for time to turn her offer over in my heart, to make a decision.

In this lifetime of sisters, threaded together by discussing every domain and detail of our lives, it was the most extraordinary conversation I'd ever had with her. Until one that would come many years later. As it turned out, I said no. Thank you from the bottom of my heart and soul, but no. Single for years following the divorce, I never felt quite sturdy enough to have a child alone. And much later, Tony came along, bringing two wonderful children of his own.

And it was easy for me to know how to love them because from the start, Kathy and Greg had welcomed me into a hands-on role in their boys' lives. I had embraced and reveled in the family-honored role of aunt and loved Patrick and Liam like they were my own. Across the years an easy, affectionate, and playful relationship with them grew.

One steamy August day in the Berkshires, I told the

boys—then ages seven and four—that I was taking them on an adventure. I buckled them into my little gold Toyota station wagon, and we drove to the Green River in nearby Williamstown. We sat in the soft grass on the riverbank eating popsicles and stuck our bare feet into the river to keep cool and watch the minnows gather to nip at our toes.

With all our similarities, we sisters had our differences. Kathy was prompt, neat, and orderly, while I was rather disorganized, given to losing things, and apt to get absorbed by minnows and little boys and to show up late for dinner. That night, Kathy stood with her hands on her hips, half smiling and half scolding me about the food going cold, and I think the boys were more entertained seeing their Mom giving me, and not them, what-for than they were by our afternoon by the river.

"I had everything ready! It's all gone cold now. If you say you'll be back by five, why can't you be back by five?" It was a long-standing question between us. I understood her exasperation. I got exasperated with myself. That yin and yang of our styles was a lifelong pattern, leading to the only times in our adulthood that I can remember her being angry with me.

Most of the time, it was just easy. Some of our simplest and happiest times involved our sitting side-by-side on the sofa, a kid on each of our laps, doing nothing more than eating up every scrap of their delicious little-boy-ness. After I moved to Boston, Kathy and her family became regular visitors to my various homes in the city. Together, we explored all Boston had to offer little ones, from the Children's Museum with its floppy rubber chickens, to Fourth of July fireworks on the banks of the Charles, to baseball games at

Fenway Park, back before most of the seats had been claimed by corporations.

Kathy, Maureen & the boys, Cape Cod, 1985.

So, it was through Kathy and Greg's open-heartedness that I was given one of the great gifts of my life, my relationship with their sons. Still, the memory of her offer is a gem tucked into my heart, a treasure of her loyalty and love. My grief over a lost baby and ultimately, the lost dream of having my own child would soften over time and became a bittersweet companion, like a heart-shaped stone I silently turned over in my pocket. It was only much later, in a way I could never have foreseen, that I recognized how not having children of my own would make it possible for me to be there unconditionally for Kathy's, when the time came.

So yes, as I watched Kathy dozing in the infusion room, there was no doubt in my mind about who was the lucky one.

The Week Time Stopped

It was mid-June before I noticed that the calendar in our kitchen was still stuck in April; a sign of how utterly preoccupied we had been by the events of Kathy's illness. The lovely but hard days of May had turned the corner into June, and the late afternoons were gifting us with a string of long golden evenings. On one of those evenings, I grabbed a handful of chives from the garden. Their peppery aroma rose from the cutting board as I chopped them for a salad. I was eyeing the twittering grosbeaks that fluttered in and out of the dogwood tree outside the kitchen window when the phone rang. It was Kathy. "They got the biopsy results back," she fired off, wasting no time on our usual chitchat. "It's Stage IV." Stage IV, which meant it had metastasized to several locations in her body. Meaning the worst.

The news was a punch to the gut, knocking out my breath and my speech. I pushed my cutting board aside and stared out at the tree. Pale ivory blossoms lifted and fell on the breeze as a wave of nausea came over me. While I went mute, Kathy continued, summarizing the devastating conversation she'd just had with Dr. Spector. A "not-your-garden-variety" version of the disease, he'd called it. My brain began to shut down. I listened but could no longer hear. Kathy's voice carried on, so I reached for a pen, as I would hundreds of times in the coming months, and started scribbling notes. Later, I

would find the scrap of paper: *large cell, follicular lymphoma.*
Some aggressive cells and some not so aggressive. She repeated
his comment about her body scans. "You're full of it," he'd
told her. "It's all through your lymph system."

The news was worse than any of us had imagined. A bolt
of protectiveness surged through me, and I scrambled for
words to cushion the blow for Kathy and no doubt for myself
as well. I wanted to grab both of us, leap into a car, and drive
as fast and as far away from this conversation as I could.

A flashbulb went off in my head: a memory of the two of
us, aged five and four, in an afternoon nursery school run by
an order of mercilessly strict Italian nuns. I recalled a perpet-
ually dark playroom, lined with gleaming, brightly-colored
toys it seemed we were never allowed to touch, much less
play with. Mom had enrolled us—thankfully only briefly—to
stretch childcare while she took a three-to-eleven nursing
shift at the local hospital.

The nuns were uniformly tiny in stature, as if members
of a tribe of miniature disgruntled women. Cloaked head
to toe in black wool, their bonnets had incongruously fes-
tive-looking frills that encircled their perpetual frowns. Any
infraction of the rules was dealt with swiftly, harshly, and
usually physically. This was a shocking development for two
little girls whose mother, in moments of parenting extremis,
had made noises about spankings, but had no experience
whatsoever with the follow-through.

To further our confusion, one of the rules in this place
was that you needed to finish every crumb of your food and
your too-warm milk, every single time. Something about

those starving children in China. "Why couldn't they have our egg salad sandwiches, then?" we wondered, with our little girl logic.

On this particular day, Kathy was gagging, refusing to eat the smelly sandwich. I watched for the right moment and grabbed the soggy thing, holding my breath as I braced for a ruler to come down on my back. Not knowing what else to do, I shoved it into my waistband and made a dash for the trash bin, somehow managing to avoid getting caught. As early as preschool, there was that impulse to protect her. That big sister sense: What would I not do to keep her from harm?

Yet here today, the gravest of dangers loomed, and I was helpless, panicked. During our brief phone call, a shadow began to fall, the felt sense of time and opportunities already telescoping closed. Of something—that easy, taken-for-granted sense of our future together—lost, when we weren't even looking. The realization dawning, with only two words from a lab report—*Stage IV*—that nothing would ever be the same.

Fighting to stay present, I tried to focus on Kathy's voice, but only seconds later found myself drifting off again, thinking about my Mom, the boys, and Greg. How would they bear this news? How could I? But these were thoughts my mind quickly threw a wall up against. They were too red-hot with fear. Instead, I was bombarded with memories of completely unremarkable, yet suddenly precious moments. Memories of the two of us shopping or taking the boys on a road trip somewhere. Wandering Main Street in North Adams before all the shops were gone, or later, at the mall, on the lookout not so much for purchases as for the next excuse to stop for tea and dessert. Kathy and I shared a love of sweets that we came by honestly through our Mom and her sisters, and our great-aunts, Mucky and Lolly, the bakers of the family.

And talking. Always talking about everything large and small going on in our lives. I flashed ahead to the wedding that Tony and I had been talking about. He had just made a mid-life career change and had begun training to become an acupuncturist. We'd been looking forward to a big family wedding in two years, after he finished his program. I realized, instantly, that this had to change. I found myself fast-forwarding to images of a smaller wedding, and soon. With the news, everything had changed. With the news, we'd stepped into another life.

I stared at the light fading in the back yard, willing myself back into the moment. I tried to keep my voice even as I reassured Kathy that, just like we'd done with everything else in our lives, we'd take on this fight together. I told her we'd talk later, before we went to sleep. Then I hung up the phone, went to our bedroom and crumpled on the bed, letting out the tears. The neighbor upstairs must have thought, well, that someone was dying. Each time I stopped there was another wave. Tony was coming home soon from school. I didn't want to call him and have him hear the news in the middle of his class. Instead, I called my Mom, then my younger brother Kevin, who was living with his family out in Washington State, and a couple of close friends. But with each phone call, pretty quickly, there were no words.

Then I paced back and forth through the house. And cleaned the counters, the stovetop, the sink. Then paced some more. Up and down the hallway, again and again. This springtime of life-as-you-know-it shattering news had been a parade of perfect beauty, one light-filled, soft-aired day after another. All the while, the clarity and beneficence of the season's glory was belying the story unfolding within. Exquisite night that it was, I didn't want to go outside. My face didn't want to show itself out in the shining spring evening.

The next night, a letter came pouring out of me. Bordering it with photos of Kathy and her family, we printed it and mailed it off to far-flung friends and family. We asked for support and "prayer in whatever way you practice or believe." I slept that night with some feeling of relief. I was beginning to find, like the infantryman in the foxhole and the devout family members who raised me, that reaching for prayer in such moments of desperation came easily, instantly. This was a surprise, given the complicated feelings I had developed about the Catholic Church since my girlhood. Yet in this hardest of times, I found it gave my heart some ease.

Adjusting to the Impossible

Kathy and Greg made a treatment plan with Dr. Spector to pursue an aggressive program of chemotherapy and to keep it local. Berkshire Medical Center (BMC) is a teaching hospital for UMass Medical Center in Worcester and a Level III trauma center. Having such excellent care available just half an hour from home made the logistics of early treatment workable and allowed local family and friends to go to appointments with her on days when Greg could not. Early on, Greg assumed the role of chief nurse and medical record keeper. As they entered a medical office, he would stay close to Kathy until she was settled in, then he would unzip his backpack and pull out a large black binder.

With wire glasses framing his kind blue eyes, Greg is known for his even temper and infectious laugh. His laid-back dress code hasn't changed in forty years: plaid cotton button-down shirt tucked into well-worn jeans, and sneakers. He approaches life with a sense of playfulness, and while his good humor was naturally muted at times by the circumstances, it nonetheless remained largely intact through much of Kathy's illness. He always brought an invaluable touch of lightness to Kathy and to the rest of us, including the ever-changing cast of caregivers, even as he cared for her with a devotion that never wavered and only seemed to increase as time went on.

Like Kathy, he was also an eminently practical person. Early on, he came up with a system to bring order to the seemingly endless stream of incoming medical data. He would ask for an immediate summary of every doctor's appointment, test, and lab result, and file it in his growing binder, neatly divided into labs, radiology, doctors' appointments, and medications.

Kathy's illness preceded the widespread use of computerized medical records, so his system made him somewhat famous among grateful ER doctors. They would see him coming, black binder in hand, and would call out, "Oh! You're the guy with the notebook! Do you have her last blood count? What's the current dosage on her prednisone?" And while they waited for the medical records department to deliver her old chart, they'd quickly find what they needed in his bulky binder.

Meanwhile, he and Kathy tried to keep things as normal as possible for the boys at home. Kathy was able to return to her job doing home-based parenting support for the local Head Start program. Greg resumed his work as an industrial electrician for a small international company located nearby. Through his employer, he had excellent health insurance, which would turn out to be of enormous importance because, in addition to everything else, at least he and Kathy didn't need to worry about quickly mounting medical debt. Just as importantly, his work treated him with a degree of compassion and flexibility that seems rare in today's business world. As both of these benefits seem to be vanishing from work life for so many these days, they would be all the more valued as we looked back on this time.

Because of the stage of the disease, with its wide metastases, Dr. Spector introduced the idea early on that at some point Kathy would probably need a bone marrow transplant (BMT), and that we needed to begin to think about finding a donor. He described BMT as a process of aggressive chemotherapy, followed by body-wide radiation at the highest survivable dose. The goal was that the radiation would knock out any cancer cells the chemo had missed. The high doses of chemotherapy and radiation also knock out the patient's immune system, so that it will not attack the newly transplanted bone marrow. This allows the new marrow to take hold and grow.

With the transplant of bone marrow, whether previously harvested from the patient or provided by a donor, a healthy immune system is put in place. It's hoped that all of the components: the chemotherapy, the radiation, and most importantly, the new immune system that can attack any residual lymphoma cells, will work together to cure the lymphoma.

"If and when we move toward transplant, we'll be looking at one of the larger medical centers in Worcester or Boston," Dr. Spector told us. "But let's not get too far ahead of ourselves," he wound up. "We want to get chemotherapy started soon, and then we'll take things as they come."

The idea of a bone marrow transplant sounded straightforward, hopeful—simple, even. Like we had a trick up our sleeves if it was needed. In the back of my mind I began to think about how to support Kathy if a transplant became necessary, and Tony and I began to talk about how we might reorganize our lives around the possibility.

At the time, I worked for an agency that provided long-term foster homes to high-risk teens. We evaluated kids in residential care to see if they were ready to be placed in homes with committed and well-trained families. I had taken the job after ten years of hospital social work on a locked inpatient unit, where I worked primarily with adolescents. The new job seemed like "social work Nirvana" to me, because a private endowment allowed the agency to provide a high level of support to the families and kids. We made weekly home visits, took the kids to medical appointments, sat in on school conferences, held family meetings to hash out conflicts, and worked out the complexities of visits with birth families. As the icing on the cake, we got to take our kids to baseball games and bowling outings, provide music and riding lessons, throw annual agency picnics and holiday parties, and, when they were ready, help with finances for college and vocational programs. That was all part of the "up" side of the job.

The down side was that because all of our kids had been removed from their birth families due to abuse or severe neglect, they bore deep wounds from early on, so life with their foster parents, no matter how patient and understanding, could get pretty volatile. It was often intense work, not easy to do when I was exhausted or preoccupied. This presented a challenge for me during Kathy's illness, and of course is a core dilemma for anyone with an ill family member who needs to earn a living.

I looked at my savings account and began talking with the HR department at work about the still relatively new Family and Medical Leave Act (FMLA), which had been passed a few years earlier during the Clinton administration. I was relieved to learn that I would be able to take up to twelve weeks of leave—albeit unpaid—should I need it, to help care for Kathy. I had followed the news of this legislation with detached interest, thinking it was a good thing for people who needed it, and that I might one day take time off to care for my mom. Little did I know I might be needing it so soon. I got hold of an application and stepped up my savings.

Throughout these stressful early months, Kathy remained fully herself, as she would throughout the entire course of her illness. She carried herself with determination, a certain fierceness even, along with a healthy dose of her trademark dry humor. The Irish wit she inherited from my dad and his family was part of what made it such fun to be with her, no matter the circumstances. During this time, a television commercial showed basketball legend Michael Jordan in a group therapy session, turning to a fellow player and asking, "And how are we *feeling* about that?" Kathy got such a kick out of the image of the ultimate jock as a sensitive new age guy that she adopted the line. From time to time, as we waited with family members in one boring, colorless medical room after another, she would survey the scene and, doing her best Michael Jordan imitation, ask, "And how are we *feeling* about this?"—acknowledging the anxiety of the situation and piercing it at the same time.

At moments, however, her humor took a sarcastic turn against the onslaught of advice that threatened to overwhelm her. An avalanche of books and articles trumpeting cures from bark teas to Qigong masters to positive affirmations tumbled across her doorstep from various friends and acquaintances. "Really, if one more person sends me a book about how to just think happier thoughts and cure my Stage IV cancer, I think I'll barf," she told me.

She tossed most of the books onto a towering heap in her bedroom, unable to find comfort in any of them. For a woman in the prime of her life, deeply knit into her community, the mother of two adored teenage sons, and the wife of a husband she loved dearly and who was still crazy about her, any notion that she had somehow brought this on by her thoughts only aggravated her.

Desperate for hope, I, on the other hand, immersed myself in reading whatever I could find at our local new age bookstore. A book about spontaneous remissions took up residence on my nightstand, a talisman or beacon of what might be possible. There were, however, a couple of books Kathy didn't toss into her reject pile. One was a take-no-prisoners description of living through and surviving a bone marrow transplant, *Seeing The Crab: A Memoir Before Dying*, by Christina Middlebrook. I read it along with Kathy and found it terrifying in its stark description of suffering. Kathy would prove again and again throughout this ordeal that she was tougher than I was. When I asked her what she found useful about the book, she said, "Because it feels like she's just telling the truth without all the rah-rah."

We came across another book that nourished her like healthy food, *Kitchen Table Wisdom: Stories that Heal*, by Rachel Naomi Remen. The author is a California physician who wrote of her own experience living with Crohn's disease, and her work with patients living with life-altering diseases, with deep warmth and compassion. Months after first reading it, Kathy would be dozing in her hospital bed and whisper to me, "Read me something from the Kitchen Table book." That one, she loved.

In the midst of treatment, life continued. Greg had long ago nicknamed Kathy the "Little General" for her singular focus on the care and well-being of her family. The boys were keenly aware of their mother's illness and the impact of treatment on her energy while, at the same time, their teen-aged lives were busy with school, homework, sports, orthodontics, music lessons, and socializing. And, chemo or not, Kathy was determined to watch over all of it without missing a beat.

She kept up her daily routine of waking early in the morning, before anyone else was up, and padding down the stairs to put the kettle on in one of the flowered flannel nightgowns that our mom gave us both every Christmas. Kathy was never a coffee person. Good black tea was the way to start the day and the remedy for most of life's ills. It was best brewed boiling hot, in one of a collection of china cups and saucers. Her favorite was an extra-large cup, also from Mom, brought back from one of her trips to Ireland. Mom had bought identical cups for each of us, including herself, pleased with the notion that whatever life brought us and wherever we were, we could have a cup of tea "together." The cup was bone china, white with gold-leaf edging, adorned with a rose surrounded by blue forget-me-nots. Kathy took her tea like Mom did, piping hot, with just a teaspoon of milk.

Waiting for her tea to steep, she would pause to look out the old double-hung windows in her pantry. The view was a rolling slope of lawn edged by wild foliage, and above, the Berkshire Hills. Grey or white in winter, green in springtime and summer, and famous for their flaming palette in autumn, the hills were always there. Ancient and softened by time, rolling and implacable, they seemed to look down on—even to watch over—all that was happening in the valley below.

Once her tea was ready, Kathy would take her seat at the round oak dining table with the cat curled in her lap and open her leather date book. One of those page-a-day journals found in any stationary store, it was the ledger of their family life and Kathy was its keeper. The dining room table was her command center, and she used the stillness of early morning to gather herself over her family's schedule, review her budget, jot down a list of what needed doing that day, and write a few bills, birthday cards, or notes to me in Boston. With her family life firmly in hand—to be anticipated, thought through, and talked over with Greg—she took this morning time to make sure that everyone's ducks were in a row for the day.

So, when disaster struck, we took our cue from Kathy in organizing as a family. Greg, Mom, Tony, and I took on her "Little General" energy to help her fight for her life. We never called a meeting, we just fell into formation as if we had trained for this all our lives. The organizing question

was "What does she need next?" We entered into an unspo-
ken contract with one another to work as a team, to keep her
needs front and center, to pray with all our hearts for a cure,
and to spare no energy in trying to love her back to health.

The Might-Have-Beens

As Kathy navigated the beginnings of her treatment plan, I couldn't help flashing back to my own experience with cancer. At 36, following the divorce and three years after I had moved to Boston for grad school, I was diagnosed with a rare and aggressive form of cervical cancer. The doctor who called to deliver the news that September morning told me it was likely due to my exposure to DES in utero. At the time, most of my DES-related issues had been resolved—or so I'd thought—but I was still being followed by a specialist at the Vincent clinic at Mass General Hospital in Boston, where some DES research was being done. That June, they had notified me of some concerning cell changes at my annual check-up. They said they'd "keep an eye on it," and told me to return for repeat tests in six months.

Soon after, I made my annual pilgrimage to Cape Cod with a friend. It was a beloved tradition, and we settled into our rental place, an over-the-garage apartment in one of the old homes that line Main Street in Wellfleet, for two weeks of beach days in the dunes, dips in the cool kettle ponds, and rainy afternoons spent shopping, reading, and making soup. One afternoon as I walked around the compact town center, past the clothing boutiques, the general store, and the bustling outdoor produce market, I felt a strong sense of foreboding wash over me. I made my way to the calmness of Mayo beach, with its buttery afternoon light. Fishermen were coming back into the harbor with their hauls, as pleasure boaters were just heading out to catch the sunset at Duck Harbor. I sat watching the comings and goings and staring at the horizon as I explored my sudden feeling of unease. I couldn't really explain it, but when I walked back to our rental place, I told my friend, "I'm having the strongest urge. I'm not waiting for six months. When I get back to Boston, I'm going in to the clinic to get tested again."

Three weeks later, the MGH doctor called me with the test results.

"It's a very good thing you paid attention to that urge. The changes since we tested in June are consistent with a pretty aggressive cancer. It's a serious thing. We'll want to take care of this surgically, and the sooner the better. But you're going to be fine. You're going to live," he told me all in one breath.

That was the good news. The bad news was that "taking care of it" meant a hysterectomy, at the very least. He referred me to a young gyn oncology surgeon, who set a date for the following week.

I was terrified at the prospect. They wouldn't know how extensive the surgery needed to be until I was unconscious in the O.R., so I had to give my surgeon wide latitude to make the best decision, not knowing how deforming the result might be. I had already had more than my share of surgeries during my twenties, but none had involved cancer. I kept hearing the confident reassurance in my doctor's voice as he had delivered the diagnosis, yet I was left with a stew of feelings that were anything but reassured, a mixture of grief, confusion, fear, and anger. Here was my body misfiring again. Here I was once again out of step with my peer group. Here I was, at 36, with cancer. And after all my efforts to have a child, here I was signing consent forms which, at the very least, meant ending any hope of bearing my own baby, forever.

Before I was admitted to the hospital, I talked with my friend Janice. We were having lunch in a tiny brick patio outside Club Passim, the folk music cafe in Harvard Square, as I told her how swiftly things had moved from the walk around Wellfleet to the date with the operating room.

"What do you need? What could help with the fear?" Janice asked.

"I know this sounds crazy, but ... I wish I knew a Native American woman, someone with ancient medicine ways, who could call a circle and make a healing ceremony ... or I wish I could summon a team of angels to surround me before I go under the anesthesia," I answered.

Janice took a long drag on her cigarette, waved it in the air and looked me in the eye. "Well. We can do that," she said.

That's how it happened that the night before my hospital admission, nine dear friends gathered in my living room to create a healing circle for me. Janice led us in a guided meditation, then my friends took turns reading poems of blessing or speaking from their hearts.

After the circle, we shared the chicken noodle soup that had been simmering on the stove, filling the apartment with its nurturing aroma. I went to sleep that night teary with gratitude. Filled up with the love and laughter and touch of my friends, I could head off to the hospital admission the following day feeling, whatever lay before me, *held*.

The next evening, as I lay in my hospital room, the door opened and in walked Kathy and my mom, who had taken the bus from North Adams to be there. I told them about the healing circle, and as Mom sat beside me saying her rosary and Kathy helped me get ready for sleep, it felt as if they were the angel team I had wished for. They stayed until I was settled down for the night, and the next day, they were the first faces I saw when I woke up post-op to the best possible outcome. The surgery had been a complete success, a "simple hysterectomy" with clean margins.

Adjusting to this abrupt end to any possibility of childbearing was, nevertheless, a long process for me, compounded by the traumas my body had been through already. My sadness and sense of loss eventually led me to the office of my first therapist, a daylight-drenched space decorated in snowy white, from plush carpet to high tin ceiling. I arrived there with no clarity about what was wrong with me and little familiarity with this thing called therapy. All I knew was that I could no longer get through a day teaching my first graders without finding myself in tears by two o'clock, when I had always cherished settling into my rocking chair surrounded by their beautiful six-year-old faces to wind down the day reading something lovely like Dr. Seuss's *Horton Hears a Who*.

I was pretty shut down during those early therapy sessions. No one had ever explained "The Rules" to me aloud, but from witnessing the behavior of the women in my clan, I knew them cold: Irish women don't cry. Irish women are strong. Irish women can handle pretty much anything life throws at them and have supper on the table by six. And most importantly, Irish women—at least those who adhered to the rules of the Church—usually wound up churning out at least one baby more than they had in mind, and often five more.

And therein lay my dilemma. Since nothing in the churning-out department appeared to be working as it should, I found myself not only heartbroken but worse, isolated. There was not a great deal of support at the time around perinatal loss, so Kathy's presence and encouragement were lifesaving for me. I coped as best I could according to the rules of my clan, trying to buck up and keep going, and to smile at the baby showers, until the weepies began presenting themselves at the most inconvenient times and in front of the most innocent people.

I took a leave from teaching and started regularly visiting the snow-white office, where, over time, I learned a name for the sadness: grief. I learned how to better protect myself (bye-bye baby showers) and came to understand that, buffeted by loss, my marriage had withered from the inside out.

But it was not all crumpled tissues. In my therapist's office I also learned about slowing down and paying attention, not only to what might please others but also to what I might need. Here again my inner Celt had to be brought along slowly: an Irish woman has *needs*? I taught myself about walking in the woods and letting the tears have their say. I taught myself that making something—a soup, a quilt, a strawberry patch—helped. I taught myself that I could take a chance and confide in some of my people, and Kathy was my Main Person, and that it felt better, less isolated and lonely, when I did.

I learned all this early, so that when the journey with Kathy hit, I had some sense of how to keep my bearings in the harsh land of grief.

Ultimately, I was able to recognize how fortunate I had been that my cancer was caught so early. When I thought about Kathy and how she had seen various doctors in the year leading up to her diagnosis: an orthopedic consult after a fall, a dermatology consult for the bruise on her leg that wouldn't heal, it left my stomach in knots. In each case the medical workup had only gone as far as that specialty's concerns. She'd gotten an x-ray, some cream for her skin. *If only someone had run a simple blood panel*, I screamed inside my head. *If only someone had just looked at her blood.*

I was plagued for some time by the "if-onlys." And by sadness around the question of why I, who had no kids, was so fortunate, while she, who had two boys to raise, was not. Of course, there are no answers for such questions. Life doesn't work like that. And fairly soon the pace of events in the present took over, leaving little time for dwelling on the might-have-beens.

The Suck Factor

We woke one Saturday in July to one of those blessed New England summer mornings, the sky a cloudless blue dome and the air, even seven miles from the shore, smelling of the sea. Kathy and her family were visiting and, unable to resist the exquisite day, we packed up and set off for the Gloucester shore.

Within the hour, Kathy and I were standing in the surf at Good Harbor Beach, surely one of the loveliest of New England's many lovely beaches, with its curved expanse of sand and tidal estuary flowing out into the Atlantic. On one side of the beach, the craggy coastline is capped with great 19th-century homes that sit above the surf like so many wedding cakes. On the other side, a riot of colorful umbrellas, towels, and sunbathers dotted the length of the shoreline. The sea was wearing its summer-best sequined blues as the waves broke softly at our feet. The sound of splashing mingled with the rise and fall of voices, the delighted cries of children, and the drone of the advertising plane overhead.

On any normal beach day, Kathy would be slathering on some coconut-scented lotion and settling her body into the warm sand for an afternoon of happy tanning. But she was two months into her first round of chemo and had strict orders to block the sunlight. Her body was pale and delicate-looking in a simple black suit, her head wrapped in a colorful scarf to protect her small skull, now denuded by the chemo.

Her neck was where the frailness revealed itself most. Her long neck was so thin, the skin nearly transparent, as if treatment had stretched it. Her shoulders were knobby from weight loss, and in the hollow beneath her collarbone on one side was a lumpy bandage covered with a waterproof dressing. The bandage covered a plastic "port" in her upper chest, a semi-permanent device implanted to spare her some of the thousands of pricks and punctures during treatment. When they removed the port, a scar would remain. As we stood knee-deep in the water, Kathy watched the boys closely, smiling at their antics and nodding for me to look. She had begun talking about how the chemo was impacting her. While she was grateful there was treatment, it was no easy task adjusting to the intrusions her body had to endure.

"I'm telling you, it's no great shakes to put on a bathing suit with this hardware sticking out of me," she said. "And then, of course, I can't be in the sun too long because of the drugs. Those chemo nurses really know how to cramp a girl's style." Then her voice softened: "But I still want to come to the beach. I love bringing the boys. That's my reason to come now, just to watch them."

Walking the treatment path close beside her, I could see the losses she was weathering each day. Seemingly small losses, that chipped away at the you you used to be. This latest one, the simple joy of her body basking in the sunshine and turning a mellow golden brown. Now, the sun, the basking, was a problem to be managed. I stood elbow-to-elbow with her and just listened, holding a beach umbrella to shield her as we stared out into the glittering sea.

We ate an easy picnic of tuna sandwiches and potato chips, sitting beneath the cabana that Greg had thrown up for shade. As we ate, we watched Patrick and Liam wrestling and cavorting in the surf. In the silence, I could feel her grief over the tracks the illness was leaving on her body and her heart, as well as her love for her sons and the satisfaction she took in maintaining as much of their normal boyhood as she could. While the grief was real, the love loomed larger. It was her engine, the driving force that was steering her treatment decisions and carrying her through whatever it took to have as much time with them as she could. Walking the way of cancer, we were learning, is a crazy-making dance of polarities: avoidance and truth-seeking, fear and love, grief and courage.

Later that month, Tony and I were able to slip away for a weekend to Wellfleet on Cape Cod. For two precious days, we were in one of our favorite places on the planet, by the sea with comfortable beds, fresh salt air, and sunshine to restore us. I spent an afternoon in an Adirondack chair facing the bay, taking in the beauty like it was medicine. I was pondering what my new therapist had said to me at our last visit. I had begun seeing her to seek help with the sleeplessness, sadness, and anxiety, which had become constant companions with cancer in the family. No stranger to loss herself, the therapist had asked softly, as if inviting me to at least consider the possibility: "What if Kathy does die?" And I had barked at her, "She can't. You don't understand. She can't." That's all I had. That was as far as I could go. Because the truth was, I could not in any way imagine my life without her. None of us could.

So it was that I found myself near sunset in my beloved Wellfleet landscape, sitting by the mudflats as the tide came in and staring into the luminous marsh. Like the day at Good Harbor Beach, the scene before me offered nothing but beauty. And yet clouds were gathering, not on the horizon but in my heart. I was trying on how to live with the prospect that had taken up residence in the middle of my chest, coloring every moment like the sun's rays shimmering over the electric-green grasses, which, in the next hour or so, would fade and be gone. I wasn't yet able to name the thing that had lodged in my chest, but the sunset on the marsh was holding a mirror up to what was unfolding in my life. All that came to me in the moment was: *I don't know how to do this.*

Everything You Never Wanted to Know About Bone Marrow Transplant

Maureen & Kathy (wearing the hated wig), Christmas, 1996.

Kathy continued her chemo. She got a wig and her hairdresser, an old friend, helped her fine-tune the style for her small face. Driving home from the appointment, her slightly chippy sense of humor was intact.

"She tells me it's easily washable!" Kathy said. "So I asked her, 'Great, can I throw it in with the towels?'"

She wore the wig a handful of times, then met me at the door one day with the chestnut curls hanging off one finger, looking like a lifeless puppy.

"Um, this thing has gotta go, don't you think? Can everyone live with that? Because I can't take feeling like I have a piece of wall-to-wall carpeting on my head." She ditched it after that for the comfort of flannel caps, covering her head in soft, flowery fabrics.

We all began to adjust to this impossible new reality: wigs and no eyebrows and days featuring a sick stomach and cold compresses for the eyes, and the new companion of constant fatigue. Tony and I got out to North Adams as often as possible on the weekends. In a pattern that persisted throughout Kathy's illness, I found myself much more anxious apart from her, and calmer, more able to focus, at her side.

We were not the only caretakers, by far. Given her age, Mom was content to have Greg or me accompany Kathy to her many doctor's appointments. She had her hands full already, visiting my dad two or three times a week at the nursing home. But she contributed to Kathy's care closer to home by cooking dinner or being there after school for the boys when Kathy was at BMC having treatments.

In addition, Kathy and Greg's community, the small town that would support them through this siege, had also mobilized, and three nights a week, warm Pyrex dishes of comfort food began arriving at the front door. Acts of love. Acts of grace. Acts that said regularly, and with brownies on the side: *You are not alone with this.*

Kathy called one afternoon after a visit with Dr. Spector. Until now he had largely left the transplant option sitting out on the horizon, introduced in theory only, while she undertook the initial months of chemotherapy. Kathy's relief about letting the transplant idea take a back seat had to be balanced against the risk that should her cancer return, and return aggressively, she could find herself too ill to qualify for it. Over the summer, the weight of this gamble had begun to shift. "Well, plans are changing!" she announced on the phone. I could picture her perched on one of the oak dining chairs that she always dragged to the pantry so that she could look out at the hills while we chatted. "Much as I don't really want to 'go there,' Dr. S. was talking today about how finding a donor—if you end up needing one—is so important. And it can take a while. Like, maybe we should use this time while things are quiet to get the ball rolling."

Part of me was secretly relieved. Getting Plan B underway suited me just fine.

"So, his office has made an appointment for us at UMass Medical Center in Worcester," she continued. "We'll meet with the team there and hear what they have to say. He says we can't even be sure that they'll consider me a candidate until they review my case, he but thinks they will."

The visit was set for the following week. Kathy asked, "Can you and Tony come? Do you mind? I can't remember half of what they say, and I don't think Greg can either."

"Are you kidding?" I answered. "If you hadn't asked, we'd have barged in anyway."

At the medical center, we found Kathy and Greg, tea and coffee already in hand, waiting by the gift shop with two sleepy-looking kids. It was already steamy at nine o'clock in the morning, overcast and oppressive, and they greeted us in khaki shorts and T-shirts. The hospital lobby was busy, and we were guided to our destination in Oncology by a heavy-set woman volunteer who warmly told Kathy what handsome boys she had. Kathy beamed, pleased, and I wanted to kiss the woman. Over and over during this journey, I found myself blessing the simplest kindness of people along the way. We left Patrick and Liam with their books by the TV in the waiting area, then we were shown into a small, airless conference room. The team was gathered at a long table, with a young physician at the head.

Greeting us wearing a surgical mask, Dr. Kelley was small and serious. She had a stash of notes in front of her, which she slouched over as if she was already exhausted at the start of her day. "I'm sorry about the mask," she began, the reason for it obvious from the congestion in her voice. "We have a lot to cover today. We want to outline the process of transplant, and even begin some testing to see if we have a family marrow match." It was a long meeting, dense with medical terminology and details, mostly of life-and-death gravity. They were more than receptive to Tony and me being involved, and in fact, because the road back from transplant is so arduous, they emphasized that family involvement would be crucial.

In teaching mode, Dr. Kelley told us that in the world of bone marrow transplant, the marrow match is all-important. For the donor marrow to not be rejected by the body, it must be of the closest possible makeup to the patient's own. But matching marrow is far more complex than matching blood types. The best chance for a good outcome would be with a biological family member, where the marrow was most likely to be genetically matched to a number of markers they referred to as HLA or human leukocyte antigens. I was growing more worried as I listened. "So, what happens if we don't have a family match?" I asked. "Without a family match, we turn to the worldwide registry to search for the closest possible match. That can be a lengthy process, which is why it's important to begin exploring the options," Dr. Kelley said.

Kathy's face was tense with listening. She sat erect, her back not even touching her chair as if her very spine was on alert. She too had notes in front of her. She'd done her homework. So much was at stake. She had recently had lunch with a North Adams woman who had undergone a successful bone marrow transplant in Boston. So, right from the get-go, she had a more realistic idea of what she might be undertaking than we did, and her questions followed suit. She worked through her list without blanching or tearing up, but pushing through. The boys weren't present, so she pulled no punches. "Tell me about the downside. What are the risks?" she asked, leaning forward.

Dr. Kelley fought a bit with her cold to keep her voice audible. "One of the risks in any transplant is that the immune system will reject the transplanted organ. However, in bone marrow transplant, it is a major part of the immune system itself that is being transplanted. So, one of the big risks here is that the new marrow will see the patient's body as foreign and launch an attack against the patient's own tissue in the liver, skin and/or GI tract. It's a condition known as graft-versus-host disease or GVHD."

Symptoms of GVHD could occur at any time following a transplant, with outcomes that ranged from the chronic-but-treatable to the lethal. The better the match, the lower the odds of GVHD. Thus, the urgent hope for a family match. Dr. Kelley concluded that they currently did transplants at UMass Medical Center only with a family donor. Without a family donor, and with subsequent higher risk, they would refer Kathy to the Dana-Farber Cancer Institute in Boston.

It was an exhaustive and exhausting interview. All along, Kathy had communicated that she dreaded the prospect of a bone marrow transplant. Dreaded it. Earlier on, in my desperation about the severity of her diagnosis, I had naively urged her: "Let's go for the transplant!" I was pinning so much hope on this option, and was still so ignorant of the cost. She, however, was not. We were handed booklets of information in chunky packets. "Everything You Never Wanted to Know about Bone Marrow Transplant," she muttered, thrusting it under her arm. "Let's get outta here and find the cafeteria. I need some tea."

Within ten days, we learned that none of us was a match. The news was more devastating than I could have imagined, for all of us. With the high odds of her Stage IV cancer returning, it seemed likely that Kathy's only hope would be to go through with the transplant at some point. Now we knew it would be a donor from the general population—if one could even be found—and would therefore be more difficult, more perilous.

That weekend when we visited, she and I were quiet, circling one another. "So, not such hot news from Dr. Kelley, huh?" she squinted at me in the kitchen as we shucked corn. During the search, our brother Kevin and his wife had even sent cord blood from their newborn daughter, in hopes it might prove helpful. "That was so good of Kevin and Cindy to do that," Kathy said. "You can't say we aren't trying every-thing." Then, steering away from the gravity of the situation, she assured me, "Well, you know I'm in no hurry to do this anyway, so if it takes a while to find a match, I'm fine with that." I felt sure she was thinking the same thing I was: *What if it takes too long? What if by the time a match is found, she is too ill to be considered a good candidate for transplant?* But those questions were too terrifying to contemplate out loud. We went on shucking.

A Breather

During the ongoing distress of this time, my meditation practice was a lifesaver for me. It had been a part of my life off and on for many years, including during a short stint at an ashram in India. Over and over during Kathy's illness, I gave thanks for that early foundation, so that I was able to find refuge at a time when I sorely need it. But I was polygamous in my seeking of divine help. While I sat in morning meditations that had their roots in the Hindu and Buddhist worlds, I kept up my silent entreaties to Mary the Mother and, as often as I could, dashed into noon Mass at the chapel near my work.

For her part, Kathy had been reading those booklets she'd threatened to toss. As we were leaving her house one evening, she walked me to the front porch to say goodbye. Away from everyone else, she paused and folded her arms across her chest, letting me know she wasn't ready for a goodbye hug just yet. She no longer bothered with her flowered caps at home, so her head was covered in downy regrowth. She brought up a statistic she'd just read, which gave the long-term survival rate for BMT with a non-family donor as 20%. Frowning and fixing her eyes on mine, she asked, "Did you read that? What do you think? That doesn't sound so good, does it?"

My knees suddenly felt less than solid, and I couldn't keep the flat dismay I felt from streaking across my face like an unwelcome comet. In fact, I hadn't read it. We were standing on the front steps of her home, a circa 1920s cottage neatly painted white with a wide forget-me-not-blue awning sheltering the brick-trimmed front garden. There should have been cookies baking in the oven and a mom in a sunhat weeding the impatiens. Instead, there was my petite, weary-looking sister, standing with a hand on her hip and a hard question in her eyes. The frightening statistic crystalized the risk hanging over this, her next and only option, other than doing nothing. And at 44, with two growing sons, that option had never been on the table.

While Kathy continued to crunch the flood of incoming information in her quiet, hardheaded way, I was still blindsided by much of it. In the heat of the threat bearing down on her, I would look at articles relating to her illness or to clinical trials or BMTs, and my brain would begin to fog over, as if the wavy lines the road gives off in extreme heat were rising off the page into my eyes. It was so threatening that I could scarcely focus, as if I were staring into the sun. Kathy, however? She was not so lily-livered, not fuzzing out or fudging the hard places.

She was due for another bone marrow biopsy to monitor the effect of her chemo regimen thus far. Her initial biopsy had been very painful, so I was already worried in anticipation. Open to anything that might help, I consulted by phone with a woman who did Reiki, a healing practice in which a trained practitioner holds his or her hands over different parts of the body, directing healing energy to them. Its comfort is accepted enough that it has found its way into many hospital settings. This woman was a well-known teacher and practiced "sending" Reiki long distance. Fairly early in the conversation, I was in trouble. It wasn't about the Reiki, or that it was too "airy-fairy" for me. I had long ago opened my mind to the whole sphere of energy healing, figuring that we don't know the tip of the iceberg yet about how mind, body, and spirit work their dance of life and regeneration.

No, it was when the Reiki lady started talking to me about Kathy's "highest healing, whatever the outcome may be in her physical body," that I felt the dark stab of heat in my belly and began to spin out emotionally. All that "whatever" language was fine and dandy in theory, when it was someone else's little sister, thank you very much. Not mine. Not MY sister. I suppressed the urge to scream at her. *"Any" outcome to her physical body, as long as it's for her "highest good" is not what we're going for here, okay?!*

She kept talking and threw another log onto the kindling of anxiety I'd begun to feel. She said something a little too blithely about Kathy "being held in the light, whatever her soul's intention is, whether to stay here or to move on." People would do that every now and then, push past what I was ready to acknowledge, so matter-of-factly that I was left stammering into the air as they walked away. She may have been right. I'm sure she was perfectly prudent to cover all possible bases of what might happen with her healing efforts. I'm sure I've done the same thing in my own therapy work. But suddenly I couldn't wait to get off the phone with the Reiki lady.

The results of the bone marrow biopsy came back and there was good news. After about three months of chemo,

Kathy was in remission. There was nothing in her abdomen; the report looked clear. She would continue to finish her chemotherapy over the next several months, but at least we knew that all signs indicated it was working. We were thrilled. Dr. Spector continued to support waiting on the transplant. Kathy too was leaning toward waiting. "Forever!" she said, a spark of exhilaration back in her voice.

The not-so-good news: With her particular cell type, there was a 30% chance the lymphoma could return within a year. That was a high percentage, Dr. Spector said, stating the obvious. "If it does return, then we know what our plan is. Then you won't wonder if you would have been fine if you'd waited, you'll know you've got a very aggressive sucker. But you can always change your mind," Dr. Spector reassured her. "You may change it 22 times before this is over. We'll talk again."

For the moment, Kathy was simply relieved to have the transplant discussion off the table. We stopped for lunch at one of our favorite Italian places, a hole-in-the-wall near the hospital that we'd frequented since we were teens. In spite of the fact that the cooks in our family were Irish—or, we'd laughed, perhaps because of this—Italian had always been our comfort food of choice. The décor in the place was timeless: old-school red checkered tablecloths, a neon Budweiser sign in the window, and dusty Chianti bottles above the bar holding candles that hadn't been lit in a decade—all of it filled with the scent of garlic. We were giddy with relief. Kathy ordered her first beer in months to celebrate, and we enjoyed a good dose of pasta and red sauce with a side of meatballs. We toasted the good news. "I'm gonna have hair for Christmas, Maureen. A little pixie cut." We clinked glasses. "And I'll be feeling better," she said, as if promising herself.

Learning that Kathy was in remission was a massive relief for all of us. It made it seem possible that this might just be it—for a long while, or even better, for good. Grateful, we all turned back to our "normal," as in not-completely-organized-around-cancer, lives.

I thought about the letter we had sent months ago to friends and family, asking for prayers. We had followed up with periodic notes to people about how Kathy was doing. Little did I realize at the beginning how important this cast of unseen supporters would become to us. As we began to get feedback, we learned that several people had shared their letters with others and as a result, she was being prayed for in many places, by circles of people she had never met. Over time, we became convinced that their prayers were holding us, giving us strength and carrying us through all that was going on. Now it seemed that the efforts of the medical team and of Kathy's many supporters were bearing fruit, and our collective prayers were being answered. I went home and gratefully wrote the newest update.

Balm for the Heart

Amazingly, throughout the whole nightmare, and side by side with it, there was also, if it can be said, such joy. That wedding that we'd had to move up? It turned out to be a life-giving project for Kathy and me to focus on. With Tony absorbed in school, Kathy needed no encouragement to sign on as my wedding-planning sidekick.

"You know how much I loved 'Four Weddings and a Funeral!'" she reminded me, recalling our afternoon watching the film while she was undergoing one of her first treatments. "I love the clothes, the music, Hugh Grant, the whole thing!" she enthused. "And everybody loves a romance with a happy ending, right? It takes me away for a little while, from what's going on with me. So, Tony is your happy ending. Count me in. I'm your official assistant!"

There were other sources of comfort as well. Months into Kathy's illness, I had found myself operating in a state of profound fatigue brought on by the anxiety, care-taking, and travel that comes with cancer in a family, alongside my sometimes high-adrenaline job. I began having regular acupuncture treatments and was quickly amazed by how deeply restorative the work was. I don't think I could have survived that time without those weekly treatments and the kindness of my acupuncturist.

The ancient Chinese medicine was changing Tony's life as well. He had been considering a career change after years working as a contractor, and knew he wanted something in the health or healing arts field. Even before Kathy's illness, he had witnessed me leaving the house wan and bedraggled from work stress, only to reappear after an hour on the acupuncture table, clear-eyed, rested and energized. Impressed, he began asking me, "What the heck is she doing for you during this treatment?!"

With my acupuncturist's encouragement, he came to a few of my visits to observe. Thus began his fascination with the world of Eastern medicine, and after exploring other options and weighing his decision, he enrolled that fall at the New England School of Acupuncture.

Maureen at Turtle Studios.

Another place of comfort during this time was the art studio/cooperative that I had joined just before Kathy was diagnosed. The studio soon became a refuge. A nondescript industrial building with beat-up hardwood floors, Turtle Studio occupied two great rooms lined with windows where a group of more than 20 artists and others like me, who still considered themselves aspirants, came to make things, often gathered around studio founder, the artist and coach Kate Ransohoff. Having joined the previous spring, I was still trying to figure out what I was doing there. But I was drawn back again and again by the beauty of these (mostly) women coming together to support one another as art-making of all kinds—painting, sculpture, writing, clay work, music, movement—bloomed around us.

Kate's philosophy put play front and center in the creative process. Thus, the studio resembled a kindergarten for adults, stocked with fabrics, glass beads, rocks, feathers, seashells, wooden blocks, dried beans, ropes, threads, and buttons, along with the usual assortment of art-making supplies. Over weeks of coming and playing, or "getting your hands in the materials and moving things around," as Kate would say, something began to happen. She pointed out that at the center of most of my studio "playing" sat a basket of yarn. She handed me the basket one day and sent me home with it, telling me, "A basket of YARNS, Maureen! I think you've got stories that need telling!"

And so, over time, in addition to the journaling I had always done to work out the questions of my life, another sort of writing began oh-so-shyly to show up. Out of the blue, poems began to arrive, fully formed, a puzzling development since I had not been a poetry reader. I was quite timid about these creatures, amazed at their appearance, yet there they were, coming through my ear like dictation. And next thing I knew, a story began to show up.

Kate Ransohoff & Maureen.

I had begun writing the story as still another way to distract myself from the often distressing days at the hospital. On one of those days when I found myself just about facedown with sadness, I had an idea. Now, I am not much of a reader of romance novels, but the notion crossed my mind, perhaps because I was deeply in love and in the midst of planning a wedding. What better way to take a break from the gut-wrenching worry, than to write myself a nice little romance, totally as my own escape? Things moved pretty quickly from there. I was standing in the shower shampooing my hair when I received the first few paragraphs of the story in my ear, just as clearly as if I were listening to Ira

Glass on National Public Radio. I got out of the shower and started to jot it down.

The romance—or initial lack thereof—involved a head-strong and vivacious woman named Rosalinda, and the deer-in-the-headlights object of her affection, a Vietnam Vet named Ernie, who thought he had his quiet life all buttoned down, thank you very much. The setting: a small down-on-its-luck mill town where he runs a Church-sponsored soup kitchen she comes to volunteer at. So, around the edges of my life, when I was at the art studio, or in the early mornings at home when I wasn't offloading the current worries of the day into a journal, I began writing, in a way that, like the poems, often felt more like "downloading." The story began to bloom into a novel: *Lunchtime at Mercy Kitchen: A Soup Kitchen Romance.*

To scout out possible wedding sites, I began driving all over western Massachusetts, arriving one day in the state's smallest town, the tiny hamlet of West Hawley. There, I found a place that felt perfect: a funky mountain-top cross-country ski center, oddly named Stump Sprouts. It was an autumn day when I visited, and as I drove the winding road along the Deerfield River, it began to snow. Amid the cascade of white tumbling from the sky, a creature stepped in front of my car: a coyote that stopped dead in its tracks, turned, and locked eyes with me before slouching back off into the squall. It felt like a strange omen. I kept driving, seven miles along the snaking river, and then a mile straight up, over the crest of West Mountain Road.

I stepped out of my car and saw the lodge, perched at eye level with the mountaintops, looking as if it were encased in a life-sized snow globe, with enormous white flakes tumbling wildly against the remnants of fall's red and gold foliage. I phoned Tony to describe it, knowing that this was the place we had been looking for.

Excited, I brought Kathy to see it, and she instantly saw how it offered just the balance of informality and beauty we'd been hunting for. We strolled around the gentle hillside, taking in the views and imagining a day many months hence. She stopped at one point to put her arm around me

"It's perfect. It's you and Tony. I can just see it, it's gonna be beautiful." I exhaled and felt a rush of happiness, feeling, as I had many times before, that everything was better after we'd seen it through both of our eyes. Once Tony had visited and also loved the funky place on the mountain-top, we set the date, a year sooner than we had previously planned.

August 9, 1997 would be our wedding day.

Autumn, 1996

Tea from China Cups

Kathy was a fan of holidays great and small, and loved their various decorations and embellishments. Her front door was adorned with a changing display of lambs, tulips, leprechauns, and wreaths as the seasons of the year paraded past.

Over Labor Day weekend, she and her family joined us in Arlington for one last beach day of the summer. After trekking home from the beach and showering off the salt and sand, we started readying for dinner. While Tony and Greg fired up the grill and the boys napped on opposite sides of the sofa, Kathy stood in the doorway of the dining room, chewing her lip in concentration.

"Hmmm. We need some decorations, don't you think?" This last was a rhetorical question. She surveyed the table. "What kind of decorations should we have for Labor Day?" she wondered. We kicked it around. Tiny strike posters? Cutouts of men in tank tops and hardhats? Her relief at being in remission and having a normal Labor Day weekend showed up in her voice.

"What about a hammer and sickle? Nah, too Communist," she decided. "Oh well," she said finally, "let's keep it simple." Setting to work at the table with a black Sharpie, she inscribed each person's napkin with "Happy Labor Day!"

Only two weeks later, Kathy was admitted to Berkshire Medical Center with a sudden onset of respiratory distress.

My initial relief—the still naive sense that if she was in the hospital, they would quickly sort it out and fix it—gave way to disillusionment when the lung specimen they took from her was lost by the lab. And things only went downhill from there.

Two days after her admission, Kathy was moved to the Respiratory ICU, where the team came in to talk with her. Along with residents and nursing staff, there were two specialists—the chief and assistant chief of pulmonary medicine. They were very kind and obviously very worried.

They needed time to diagnose the problem, they told us. Her pulmonary status was deteriorating rapidly, so they wanted to place her on a respirator briefly to buy time and run their tests. Kathy was terrified, as were we, but the doctors were pressing to act immediately. They asked Greg, Tony, and me to step out of the room. "It will only take a few minutes to intubate her," they told us. "It will be fine."

We returned half an hour later. It was definitely not fine. Kathy's face had a look I had never seen before. Her eyes were wild, her skin was clammy and so pale it was nearly transparent. And blotchy, as if she had been crying or struggling somehow. She couldn't speak with the tube in her throat, so we settled around her bedside, stroking her arm trying to calm and reassure her

The following day, the pulmonary specialist asked to speak with us again. It was her second day on the respirator and things were not going in the right direction.

The studies thus far were inconclusive. Perhaps it was an unusual infection. Perhaps it was a reaction to one of the chemo medications. Perhaps it was viral or fungal. The treatment of choice for one problem, such as steroids, could worsen matters exponentially if the diagnosis was one of the other problems. The treatment decisions they needed to make required still more testing. They wanted to take her to the OR to do something called an open lung biopsy. Immediately.

Afraid that I wouldn't be able to remember what they were saying, I dashed off notes from the consult: *O₂ level continues to fall/ need to make incision in chest/ sample from each lung. Should take 1/2 hour.*

Fairly quickly into being intubated, Kathy had begun gesturing for paper and pen and weakly scratching out note after note, keeping up a flurry of questions and commentary. When I turned over the piece of paper I'd grabbed for my jottings, I found something that she had written to me earlier, her pencil marks so faint they were scarcely readable.

As usual, her people skills had been at work. *The nurse? Hannah? She is having treatment for cancer, too. Breast,* she wrote. Then: *She's a great person. She has two little kids, girls.*

Before they took her downstairs for the biopsy, she scratched out another note: *Patrick's class picture appointment. Saturday at 10 a.m. Drop sport coat at dry cleaners in time.*

True to form, even on a respirator and on her way to have someone cut open her chest, she was fretting that her boy might have a spot on his jacket for his class photo. Amazingly, frustratingly, the biopsy was also inconclusive.

Her oncologist had thought all along that Kathy was having a reaction to one of the drugs in her chemo cocktail, something he'd read about but had never seen clinically. Grasping at this hypothesis because they had little else to go on, they began a trial of IV steroids. And Kathy started to improve.

We were massively relieved, while frustrated that three days had been lost in looking for answers. Days of suffering for Kathy. Days when her body and organ systems were being taxed and precious strength was sapped that she would need later in the battle. And it wouldn't be the first time we would be sobered to witness how very trial-and-error the "science" of medicine could be, up close.

When it came time to wean her from the respirator, the specialist doctors were not around. We dealt with a chief resident, who compensated for his limited experience with an abundance of arrogance. I took him aside in the hallway and begged him to give her something to help calm her through the procedure, given how badly the intubation had gone. "Please. She was completely traumatized," I pleaded to the doctor.

As I later raged to Tony about the doctor's response to my request, I recognized that there might have been good reason not to medicate her, so as not to further depress her respiratory system. If he had only explained that to me, I would have understood. I would still have pushed to see if other medication options were available, but I would have understood.

The chief resident, however, deigned to explain nothing to me, and communicated only annoyance. "This will be nothing!" he snorted, disappearing into Kathy's room, as the door slammed behind him.

Once again, half an hour passed, and we entered to find many more people leaving than the procedure should have taken, including a specialist they had needed to page, STAT.

The tube had been very difficult to remove. "Her airway is so small!" a worried-looking nurse gently explained.

As we reached Kathy's side she whispered to Greg and me, "I will never do that again. Never. No more respirators. No matter what. Promise me."

We promised.

Over the next week, her breathing improved rapidly, thanks to the steroids, and she was discharged home. Amazingly, within weeks she had regained enough ground to return to her job, providing parenting support through Northern Berkshire Childcare. Finally out of the respiratory crisis and still in remission, she was still sitting with the likelihood, given her Stage IV diagnosis, that the lymphoma would return and at some point, in an attempt to save her life, she would need the bone marrow transplant.

While Tony was in school at night, studying acupuncture meridians and the ancient ideas behind them, I was coming home during this difficult time to an empty house. I sometimes distracted myself after work by roaming in stores. One evening, I found myself at 7:30 in one of the chain stores, wandering almost in a trance, as if avoiding something. Suddenly I caught myself, and thought, *Get me OUT of here!*

I bolted to the car, a wave of feeling rising in my chest. Anger. *Why is this happening?* I wanted to scream. I recalled the story that our Russian moving guy Maks told us when we were preparing to move into our Gray Street home in Arlington. He had phoned to say he would be out of the country and we wouldn't be able to reach him for the two weeks preceding our move. His best friend, the fellow he had grown up with in Russia, had died at 35, and Maks was returning home for the funeral.

Later, after his return, we asked him how he was doing. He told us that once the funeral was over, he had taken his sleeping bag and a bottle of vodka and gone off into the woods. "Far, far away from everyone," he said in his thick Russian accent, "where I could stay alone and make noise and scream and not disturb." He stayed out there for a week, he told us, until he felt done.

I got it completely. It seemed like the only sane response, and exactly what I felt like doing: going out into the forest and wailing at the sky. Instead, I found the woods near our house for the hundredth time and walked. Hard. And cried. I was angry yes. And beneath it was a terrified sadness.

As I coped with the anger I was experiencing I found again that writing my way through it helped.

Journal: October 4, 1996

Going through two hell weeks at work. Everything is a blur. One kid was expelled after a knife was found in his backpack, then he came clean that he's been snorting his meds. Then, two brothers blew out of their foster home due to bad behavior, and we had to find immediate placement for them. The school called an emergency meeting to discuss them at 7 a.m. this morning!

Emergency. Everything right now feels like an

emergency. And I have zero reserves to deal with them. Waking at 3 or 4 a.m., so handling it all with bone-deep fatigue and anxiety, And beneath all that, this rage. Rage because my sister is so sick, and I don't even know where to put my fear about that. And I don't know how to carry the work stress and the worry at the same time. Struggling with feeling like I have nothing to whine about—it's Kathy who is so ill. And yet just feeling flattened and stuck.

How do I handle it all differently for the long haul? How on earth to make it all more "handle-able"? How do we be alive while feeling this crushing stress? Though, oddly, even as I am writing, there is a space that begins to open up, some breath I can catch. I've been reading so much Stephen Levine, I begin to hear him in my head (Oh, thank you Stephen!) He writes about "cultivating a merciful awareness." I so love that word. Mercy. From that vantage point, my better angels might counsel: "You are all bearing this very hard thing very well. It is a great gift that you love your sister and her family so. Your grief is precious and human. Feel what you feel, and try not to judge yourself badly for feeling it."

The date for Kathy's bone marrow biopsy arrived, followed, as always, by worried waiting. So much of living with cancer is worried waiting.

But Kathy's wry humor prevailed, as did her doctor's, when they did the biopsy, which involved a king-sized needle and her hipbone. It was Halloween, and as promised, Dr. Spector had appeared for office hours in a Frankenstein costume.

"I guess you have to have a sense of humor to survive in his line of work," Kathy's voice sounded fond and amused, telling me about it. "I told him just so long as he doesn't come near me with that long needle dressed like Dracula!"

Another month went by. I continued to sit and meditate around dawn each morning because I could not sleep. One morning, I sat for nearly an hour after waking early. I smiled to myself, remembering the chat I'd had the evening before with Kathy.

She had told me that she too, had been waking up at four a.m. We joked about calling each other in the wee hours, and remembered how as kids, we had held "Night Hawk" sleepovers on our cousin Susie's front porch. We were in eight- and nine-year-old heaven in our matching Dutchmaid bathrobes, staying up late outdoors in our PJs, with Cokes and Appian Way pizza my Aunt Alice made from a box mix.

Kathy chuckled that we'd moved on from Night Hawks to Insomniacs. "We should start having phone meetings at four in the morning! Let's call Susie and see if she's up, too. I don't know who's gonna make the pizza, though."

My heart ached at the thought of her sitting at her dining room table in the pre-dawn hours with her cup of tea, alone with her thoughts. Kathy had been a worrier from way back. It was part of her high-strung nature. So, Lord knew what was going through her head at four in the morning.

I found myself hoping she was praying. I found myself praying she was hoping. I found myself imploring God—Whoever, Whatever is out there—to help her find her way to some comfort.

I was grateful that among my many sources of comfort—Tony, my friends and family, acupuncture treatments, meditation, writing—I still had a sense of a Someone or Something, of God, of grace, that I'd never really lost no matter how estranged I'd felt from the institutional Catholic Church. And I tried hard to reach out, or inward, to that. In moments of desperation, I surprised myself with the urge that arose—it felt, from my very cells—to pray. In such moments, there seemed no other way than looking to God or Mother or Spirit, however you name it.

I shouldn't have been surprised. Growing up on the street our grandparents, aunts, uncles, and cousins lived on, and in and out of each other's homes every day, there had never been any question that family occupied the center of our universe. But the foundation, the ground beneath our family, was a devout Irish Catholic faith. My parents were not unquestioning Catholics, nor were they evangelical. But they were, truly, authentically devout. Prayer and often daily Mass was a real part of their lives, a source of comfort and belief.

As long as she lived, my mother brought every trouble in our family to her rosary or her novenas, a set of prayers and petitions said for nine consecutive days to the Blessed Mother or to one of the saints. And I can still see my Dad, his tall frame folded into the living room rocker, his thin shoulders hunched over his worn leather prayer book. His favorite saint was Francis of Assisi, which made sense, given his love of animals of all kinds. Our schooling, from primary through high school, was with the Sisters of St. Joseph. When my grandmother installed a then state-of-the-art black and white television in her living room, we sat around it on Sunday nights watching Bishop Fulton Sheehan as if he were Ed Sullivan.

Mom & Dad having tea, 1981.

So, steeped in a family of faith, I found myself becoming a prayer machine. *Help me. Help her. Oh please. Help her. Her, and the boys and Greg. To find a way to You. To find comfort and hope. To be healed. Healed. Please.*

But I was not only begging in my prayers. I also found myself feeling supremely grateful for moments when things were going well, when we could see some light, and easily moved to tears by the smallest graces. At those times, another prayer arose in my chest: *Thank you, Thank you, Thank you.*

And then, there was a different sort of prayer. The moments when we got to make each other smile about our mutual insomnia and next thing you know we were talking about pizza and should we call Susie to see if she has become an insomniac, too? And how the trip to look at Syracuse with Patrick went, which was easier than the conversation about going to the doctor tomorrow.

We seized on doctor's appointments as if they were life preservers in a storm-ravaged sea. Even though, as Kathy reminded me, "Dr. S. isn't gonna be able to say anything much. It's a watch and wait situation. It's not like he has a rabbit he can pull out of his hat."

This kind of prayer was about staying present, keeping her company in this place of helplessness and uncertainty. We cried and we chuckled. We told each other stories and drank tea from china cups. All that was prayer, too. And that was how we navigated this dangerous, terrifying path.

Winter, 1996 – Spring, 1997

To Keep Us Strong

Maureen & Kathy, Thanksgiving, 1996.

The holiday season was approaching, a time that we usually loved and looked forward to spending together. But this year was colored by the specter of Kathy's illness. The ever-present uncertainty about a relapse added an undeniable strain, while at the same time immolating any sense of the taken-for-granted. The hours we spent together were thus imbued with a sharp sense of immediacy.

At Thanksgiving, we gathered in our Arlington dining room, illuminated on a sunny morning by the golden-hued stained-glass window, an architectural detail I had always loved. The house was full of Thanksgiving-morning turkey smells, made even more mouth-watering by the savory spices Greg used in the stuffing he made each year. Tony carved while my mother did gravy duty and I made a cranberry-orange sauce. The sounds of the Macy's parade could be heard from the TV in the living room, where Patrick and Liam were hanging out.

As usual, Kathy had been up early, dressed and ready to celebrate in her classic holiday best: a red V-neck sweater over a navy turtleneck, with gold bangles on her wrists and gold hoops dangling from her ears. She had donned the much-maligned wig of short curls for the occasion and looked thin but vibrant. Her manicured fingernails were rose colored, and her rings sparkled as she circled the table, fussing over details and arranging a spray of yellow roses and crimson alstroemeria in a hand-painted vase we had received as an engagement gift. "This vase is so pretty, so original," Kathy called out to me. "That girlfriend of yours is so artsy!"

I had taken a moment earlier in the day to reassure Kathy that if and when she needed a transplant, I would be able to take a leave from work to be with her as much as possible.

"How can you do that? I mean—I can't lie, I would love you to—but, how? Would work let you? What about money?" she asked.

I explained about the FMLA act, and that I had already talked with HR at work and had the paperwork in hand just in case. "And luckily, I have some savings," I told her. "I've been stashing a bit away regularly, thanks to Mom's example!

And I stepped it up last year, so I'll be good."

"And Tony...?" she asked.

"We've talked. We're all set. It's good. I'm totally one hundred percent in for doing it if we need to."

Kathy didn't say anything. We stood looking at each other for a beat. She nodded. "Thanks," she whispered.

When we gathered at the table, we joined hands and I asked my mom to say grace. Her voice wavered only a little, in the middle of her prayer. "Dear Lord, we thank you that we are here together, and for your bounty set before us. We ask your special blessing of healing and health for Kathy, and we trust in your goodness to keep us strong, Amen."

And I couldn't help but chime in, "And while we're at it let's give thanks for that Family Leave Act! Thank you, God and thank you, Bill Clinton!" We all laughed.

Just days later, we met up again in Worcester for a second transplant consultation at UMass Medical Center. The medical team there had consulted with the Dana-Farber/Brigham and Women's Hospital in Boston, and considering both the inherent risk, as well as Kathy's recent respiratory crisis, they recommended holding off on a decision about a transplant. This was what Kathy wanted, but still, knowing that she could become too weakened or too ill for a transplant, it was hard to let it go. They hadn't found a bone marrow match yet, but the search continued, in case it became necessary.

The next week, when Kathy had a follow-up appointment with Dr. Spector, I found myself once again struggling with being nearly three hours away. He might have more news from the Brigham team, and Greg couldn't go to this one, since he'd missed so much work already.

Each of these appointments took on such urgency. I desperately wanted to go with her, but I had a full day of appointments scheduled at work. I did the math in my head over and over, agonizing over the choice between driving out to accompany her for what could be an important consultation or keeping my own commitments. Neither option felt right.

It felt especially hard whenever important information was under discussion. I worried that by herself, Kathy might have trouble recalling all the details. Under this kind of stress, it's important for anyone to have another person present as back-up memory of what is said and to help process the information in real-time in order to raise questions.

It's a common problem, one that people who are ill must deal with daily. I wondered why the medical offices didn't have transcription staff on hand to take notes and send patients home with the important bullet points all typed up in black and white. Instead, they are often left to depend on others to take off from work to accompany them in this supporting role. As I saw through this complex, confusing, and emotional process, this role is both desperately important and challenging for friends and family to keep up with.

This importance was borne out during one of Kathy's hospital stays, when Greg and I were standing in the hallway outside her room with Dr. Spector and we mentioned her current dose of prednisone. He cut into what we were saying with evident alarm. "Wait! How much is she taking? I had changed her dose at her last office visit!" Kathy had been alone at that appointment, and hadn't remembered the dose correction, so she had remained on the wrong dose well past when he had made a change, with some unwelcome consequences. Remembering this incident left me even more twisted up in knots about my stay-or-go dilemma.

In my morning meditation practice, I found flashes of mercy and lightening, and I felt grateful for them. But they felt like bubbles on the surface of a river called Grief. Still, I remained grateful for other comforts. While I ruminated over a decision where neither outcome was satisfying or clear, Tony was in the kitchen cooking us some eggs. He came to the doorway to tell me breakfast was ready and caught me off guard. Fresh from my sitting, I was staring out at the treetops glistening with morning light, trying to settle in with my decision that this time, I would go to work. He spoke softly, so not to startle me and I turned to him, the stillness unbroken. A feeling welled up inside me and I breathed a little more deeply: *My heart rests in you.*

Christmas was spent in the Berkshires. For years we had brought Dad home to Kathy's for Christmas day, but he had lost ground and this year we felt taking him out of his familiar surroundings would only create more confusion for him. So we packed up his gifts and went with Mom to spend the early part of the day with him. Until we reminded him to open his gifts, he didn't even know it was Christmas. But he had moments when he rallied and was suddenly lucid. "Oh

Maureen! It's good to see you, Sweetie." Then he might ask, even while Tony stood beside him with a hand on his shoulder, "Did you bring Tony with you?" Kathy stayed home to greet the kids as they woke up, and after visiting Dad we joined them around the tree.

The two matriarchs: Mom & Eugenie, 1996.

Our family Christmas was also enriched by the inclusion of Tony's mom, Eugenie, beloved matriarch of her own large family and known by all as "Nonie." She had been following Kathy's story with concern and when Kathy invited her for the holiday, she didn't hesitate to accept. Nonie and my mom had much in common. Born the same year, both had had decades-long careers as nurse-leaders, both were steeped from girlhood in a deep Catholic faith, and both remained well into these later years, extremely sharp mentally. As Kathy and I set out the food, Mom and Nonie sat forehead to forehead under the holiday lights in the living room reminiscing and catching up on news of the two families.

The dining room was festive, with the tree set up in one corner and a cluster of Christmas stockings hanging, as always, around the doorway. Kathy was bright and happy for the occasion and was quick to raise her glass for a toast. "We have lots of gifts this Christmas, including Nonie joining us and a wedding to look forward to this year!" she said. "Tony, it took Maureen a long time to find you, but you were totally worth the wait! We're so excited about the wedding and before you two take off this weekend, I want to start looking at dates to throw you a shower!"

However, in the midst of planning our celebration, March brought another anniversary to get through, with its poignant memories from twenty years earlier when I lost my newborn daughter, Megan. The anniversary announced itself each year in my body with a sense of heaviness that I recognized as my old friend grief, resurfacing. As if my body had its own calendar encoded deep in its tissues, the physical reminders shifted in shape and intensity from year to year. Perinatal losses often become invisible. There were few people in my current Boston life who knew the story, and fewer still who were there and part of it. Kathy was one of them. The grief that still hit me at the oddest moments had a home with her.

I recognized that the grief was not only for my baby. I was also grieving for myself as a young mother, for the mother in my bones and in my cells, the young woman who braved the tests and procedures, the surgeries and the disappointments. In this anniversary season, I made space in my heart to hold her, too. I imagined waving Megan a kiss, and I felt that she was fine, in her dancing light.

I bowed inwardly in meditation to the brave young woman I was, and to her heart, repeatedly broken, but always coming back in hope. I prayed that the seeds she had planted in her new life would fall on blessed ground and grow fruit. That she would find her rightful place in the circle of her sisters. That she'd be free of danger. That she'd be happy. That she'd be at peace.

Decades after that first sad March, I could sit and begin a new journal in a time of regeneration and hope that Kathy was going to make it through this. She'd continued in remission, followed closely at Berkshire Medical Center by Dr. Spector and, except for the fatigue, was doing pretty well.

I was filled with hope as well, for a new marriage.

So while I took time to light candles in honor of the old grief, I was also occupied with new joys. My brother Kevin, who lived out in the Cascade Mountains of Washington, was planning a visit with his wife Cindy and their baby, Brenna. They were coming east for a wedding that summer. Ours.

On a too-warm Sunday afternoon in May, Kathy hosted a bridal shower for me. Her house was full of flowers and buzzing with girlfriends, cousins, and aunts. There were deviled eggs and cupcakes, champagne and strawberries. Kathy was in her element, casually dressed for the hot afternoon in a loose cotton t-shirt and shorts. She stood in the doorway, calling out to corral the group from drinks in the back yard through the sunny side porch and into the house for lunch and gifts.

"Be careful of my cat!" she warned, laughing and trying to hold onto the squirming feline, who had a tendency to reach out and biff people, but never Kathy, as they passed. "She's an attack cat! She'll swat you if you get too close!" The house rang with laughter and too many conversations happening at once. I looked up and caught her eye as she stood in the doorway, surveying her handiwork. She couldn't have looked more pleased.

Summer – Autumn, 1997

A Long Walk with Tony

Maureen & Tony with Millie and Eugenie, Wedding Day, 1997.

August came and brought our wedding day, full of light, as full as we could ever have imagined it could be, and then some. Full to the brim with beauty and sweetness, spilling out over all of us.

We traveled to western Mass and up the pitted, snaking road to the mountain lodge, and woke to the sounds of heavy trucks and pounding as sturdy men arrived to hoist the great white tent, rising like the crisp sails of a tall ship in a sea of bright green pasture.

In the afternoon, guests began arriving from all over, pouring like happy ants down the staircase into the pleasingly rustic kitchen, where we began with a meal. There were tables covered in gingham, jelly jars bursting with Queen Anne's lace and black-eyed Susans, and smells from the grill wafting through the open windows as the boisterous sounds of old friends and family reuniting rose and fell in the small space.

An evening of shared work followed, starting in some chaos, and then growing into a cloud of focused activity. Tony's sister Rosie had filled the barn with buckets of flowers and, with her helpers, made centerpieces and bouquets of blue hydrangea, peach roses, sunflowers, lilies, and delphinium. My new sisters-in-law pulled out yards of muslin, gently wrapping an archway for us to stand under as bride and groom.

After breakfast the next morning, nephews and nieces rolled up programs and set tables for the feast, as music spilled out from the loft onto the patio where guests began to gather. Flowers, programs, chairs, gold tablecloths, and yards of muslin flew from hand to hand and landed, somehow, in the very shape of the vision that had lived in our hearts, but we hadn't been sure we could even articulate. In the hands of our nearest and dearest, it all took on the shape of love, which was of course all we ever wanted.

For weeks later, Tony and I would happily recall details from the day: the plumed white tent floating in the deep green hills, laughter rising like smoke from the landscape as pods of helpers worked together like wedding elves, cowbells softly clanging from the cows grazing in the gated meadow.

And my sister loaning me her steadiness and lightness to lean on as I fretted that Tony was too busy chatting instead of getting ready and was going to be late. Just after noon,

Maureen & Kathy, 1997.

Maureen & Tony, Wedding Day, 1997.

Kathy came across the lawn to my room to fetch me. The August heat was bearing down and now it was the bride, not the groom, who was running late.

"Are you ready, bride? Let's go! The groom is waiting for you, and it's hot out there!" she coaxed as she took my hand. A friend snapped a photo from behind as the two of us walked across the lawn. We paused at the barn door and my heart caught at the sight: rows of girls, sixteen in all, in their best summer dresses, each one, from toddler to teenager, invited

Maureen and her nephews, Wedding Day, 1997.

to be a flower girl. They held hands in twos, crowned with wildflowers and ribbons, so beautiful they brought tears to my eyes. I started making my way through the rows, kissing each one until, again, Kathy's voice brought me back.

"Okay, okay! The music is starting! Let's *go!*"

Overcome with love and pride, I watched Patrick and Liam step forward and come to my side to give me away, then saw Tony make his way up the hill through the tall grass with his children, Carla, aged twelve, and Jordan, ten, one on each arm. I paused for a moment, taking it all in, while the music of Pachelbel's Canon floated over the hills. As Tony came closer our eyes met for just a beat, each of us overcome with joy at seeing all we had planned and hoped for beginning to unfold.

We had written our ceremony together with the trio of dear friends who were officiating, longtime members of our meditation group. It included an exchange of silk shawls that some friends had hand-painted for us during a pre-wedding celebration. Against the backdrop of mountains and sky, Tony tenderly placed my shawl around my shoulders, and one of the little ones erupted in a raucous whoop that brought a burst of laughter from the crowd. We turned to face the circle of loved ones as everyone raised their hands in a blessing by James Bertolino from the book *Life Prayers.*

> *May your love be firm,*
> *and may your dream of life together*
> *be a river between two shores—*
> *by day bathed in sunlight, and by night*
> *illuminated from within. May the heron*

carry news of you to the heavens, and the
salmon bring
the sea's blue grace. May your twin thoughts
spiral upward
like leafy vines, like fiddle strings in the wind,
and be as noble as the Douglas fir.
May you never find yourselves back to back
without love pulling you around
into each other's arms.

A sudden shower during the wedding meal turned the air heavy with humidity and, except for a few hardy souls, dampened the crowd's dancing enthusiasm. But, August heat or no, Kathy was in the vanguard of the hardy, out in the middle of the dance floor, arms raised above her head, shaking her booty, dancing her dance.

Later that night, famished, Tony and I crept back into the kitchen to find some leftover desert. Like most wedding couples, we had scarcely eaten three bites of the feast, after all the planning that had gone into it. So, we raided the refrigerator after everyone had gone to bed, then lay out a blanket in the meadow and ate fresh peach melba with heavy cream while watching August's Perseid meteor shower rain light down in the jet blue sky.

And took it as a token of blessing on our day.

After the Honeymoon

Journal: August 26, 1997

Back home again, and glad to be writing in the new journal given to me and inscribed by a friend: "To Maureen, who is taking a long walk with Tony."

We are home from our honeymoon on the west coast. Twelve days together, landing in San Francisco for a few days, then heading up the coast toward Tony's old haunts in Oregon, by way, inland, of Mt Shasta. Which was so peaceful and powerful, the meadow alive with wildflowers, that we got distracted from our trip north and stayed two days. Our favorite photo from the trip was taken by one of the handful of people we encountered at Shasta, and shows us huddled together, beaming, in the pouring rain. We headed, later than planned, to the Oregon coast and on to the Hood River Gorge, flying home from Seattle. Nearly every day a new place, so my journal fell out of my lap in favor of walking in the beautiful west with my new husband as he introduced me to these places where he spent nearly a decade of his life.

Tony's western chapters followed his attending seminary high school from age 13, then entering the novitiate with the Carmelite Fathers in western

Massachusetts. Recognizing even then that he longed for a family, he left the Carmelites behind at age 19, trading the monastic religious path for a life on the road. His travels took him from the Berkshires to San Francisco, then north to British Columbia and south to Mexico, working all manner of jobs from itinerant farmworker to chimney sweeper, to supervisor in an adolescent group home. As we traveled, his stories of this time came to life and I understood completely how this land in the west would have captured his heart. And indeed, it had been a moment of him telling me, glowing with the memories, of his time living on a river in a tipi out west, when I knew he had captured mine.

We had not finished unpacking from our honeymoon when we learned the news: Kathy's cancer was back. She had noticed some new swelling in late summer and had brought it to Dr. Spector's attention, but she had chosen to wait until the wedding was over to tell us.

It was clear now that a bone marrow transplant would be the next stop. Late November found us at the Dana-Farber Cancer Institute (DFCI) in Boston, where we met with a young oncologist, Dr. Stephanie Lee, to begin the arrangements for marrow transplantation. If they approved Kathy, and if she decided to go forward, Dr. Lee would be her transplant physician.

Kathy's first appointment with Dr. Lee was scheduled on a morning when a November blizzard had blown through

New England, dumping snow that measured in feet, not inches. Not wanting to postpone the important meeting, Greg calmly managed the long drive across Massachusetts through the drifting, swirling storm, and made it up the not-insignificant hill we lived on to collect Tony and me to accompany them. Already relieved just to have arrived safely, we entered the lobby in a gust of blowing snow and were greeted by the almost festive atmosphere of a workplace operating with a skeleton crew, as cheerful volunteers approached us with hot chocolate and oatmeal cookies. The stressful drive and the reason for our visit notwithstanding, our immediate impression of Dana-Farber was one of welcome, sealed with cocoa and cinnamon.

Dr. Lee found us in the quiet waiting area and introduced herself, her hair caught up in a sideways ponytail that looked like it had lost a battle with her hat. In place of the white hospital coat we would see her in often, she wore a plaid flannel shirt and corduroy jeans jammed into her snow boots. She looked like an Asian-American high-schooler ready to go snowboarding, rather than a transplant specialist at one of the world's finest cancer centers. But she quickly left us with no doubt about her expertise, her ability and willingness to communicate, and her warmth and heart. She had a way of intuiting what you might be thinking and bringing it up to be addressed. And she was not afraid to touch when she talked.

"We're going to cover a lot of information today," she told us. "It makes people's heads swirl. But you don't have to get it all today, so try to just sit back and take in what you can.

You can call later with any questions, any time. And remember, this is your decision. There is no pressure to say yes to a transplant. You have to talk together and decide what's best for you," she assured us, putting a hand over Kathy's.

It was another sobering meeting in a sobering time. The room was windowless and stuffy, as all these rooms seem to be. The faces around the table were somber, and Dr. Lee's tone was compassionate yet frank. She didn't "pretty up" the information. Bone marrow transplant was a desperately risky intervention. But, given Kathy's Stage IV lymphoma and her recent relapse after a full course of chemotherapy, it was our best shot at wiping out the cancer.

And since there was still no marrow match, time was not on our side. The search for a match would continue as Kathy and Greg weighed this next step. My old companions sadness and sleepless worry returned.

While we continued the waiting game, the fall and winter holidays rolled around again and Kathy, however fatigued, was once again game for all of it. Christmas weekend, spent at Kathy and Greg's in North Adams, was the usual flurry of four o'clock children's mass on Christmas Eve, followed by a noisy, busy gathering with our cousins, and a Christmas morning of gift-wrap flying around the living room. Then afterward, the quiet, treasured down-time together, time that we felt more sharply alive to, with all that we now knew lay ahead.

On the morning of December 26th, while Greg was busy washing the dishes after a breakfast of his famous strawberry pancakes, Kathy and I sat together, the overcast morning brightened by the twinkling lights of their tree.

"Every year we go back and forth about getting a fake tree," Kathy told me. "I know it would be less messy, but I'm not ready to give up on my fresh tree." The tree was hung, not in any sleek designer style, but family style, with ornaments that had been gathered over the years. Baseball gloves from Cooperstown, hand-glittered tracings of kindergarten hands hung with fraying yarn, photos of the boys as infants in fancy brass frames declaring "Baby's First Christmas."

As we sat enjoying the post-holiday calm, Kathy called Patrick over from whatever he was doing, and patted the space beside her on the sofa.

"So, come and sit with me. How was your practice today?" Eye contact. Attention. She was not distracted as she asked, as so many of us are these days with checking our phones, or scanning Instagram. She was sitting, arms folded over her chest, focused, as I had seen her do with her sons countless times over the years.

"Did you talk to Coach about your game the other day? What did he say?"

She was a world-class listener. When she asked you a question, she stayed present for the answer. Looking into the face of the boy beside her, she let the conversation unfold, letting the answers sink in, unhurried. She drew her boys out, her lively interest helping to give form and shape to what was happening in their lives. But that was how she listened to each of us, with her keen curiosity and quick humor.

Over and over as my life had tumbled through its darknesses, that kind of listening had been a lifeline for me. The sense that someone dear to me was tracking the baby steps I was taking to put myself back together, as if whatever I was facing was a problem that we shared and that she and I would meet, together. Kathy lavished this gift of time and focus on the people she loved, as if each chat were an occasion.

Later in the weekend, in what felt like our true Christmas gift, a phone call came from Boston. As she got off the phone, Kathy called out to me to come downstairs. I found her with Greg in the living room.

"Well, here we go," she began. "That was Stephanie Lee. They have a donor. It's not a perfect match," she continued. "It's 7 out of 8," referring to the haplotypes they were trying to match, which measure genetic compatibility. "But they feel like it's good enough to go ahead. And they have a date. It's going to be February 28th."

We all looked at one another. However nervous we all were about it, the transplant was now her only option, so learning we had a donor was huge news.

"If I'm gonna do this, then let's do it already! It isn't helping to wait!" she told us. "Now at least I can picture it, I can start to organize and get things ready."

I phoned her later that week to report in. "Well I filled my FMLA paperwork out and handed it in to HR. I'm taking 12 weeks, just in case, you know, we need it," I said.

"I'm of two minds about that. I mean, it's such a big sacrifice, who can go without pay? Are you sure you can swing it?" she asked. "Because, on the other hand, it is so comforting, I can't even tell you. That you'll be there."

"My savings account is very happy right now," I said.

"Besides, what could I spend it on that would be more important?"

"A trip!" she said. "A big trip! Or, a house."

There wasn't a trip I wanted more than a chance for her to get more time. And from that vantage point, there wasn't a house that would be much fun if she weren't around to come visit.

My leave was approved, and I felt a rush of relief. Aside from knowing that Kathy and Greg would need me, I knew also that I would never be able to concentrate at work while she was undertaking this rescue that was so fraught with risk. And I still had no real idea just how much risk she would face.

In the Tower

Bone marrow transplantation may be the worst treatment in all of modern medicine—and the best.

— Jerome Groopman, MD

While Dana-Farber is a name synonymous with cancer research and care, we were surprised to learn that there is not a Dana-Farber hospital. The Dana-Farber facility provides outpatient services, while at the time of Kathy's admission, patients needing inpatient care were admitted to one of the Dana-Farber floors at Boston's Brigham and Women's Hospital (BWH).

Kathy and Greg came to Arlington to stay with us the night before admission day. Setting out the next afternoon for the hospital, we continued to take our cues from Kathy, and it was clear that she was in no hurry. More specifically, she was stalling. Once parking was secured, we entered the bustling lobby and, following Kathy's lead, we slowed right down to a crawl. We lingered in the lobby and watched the crowds move past.

Internationally renowned, "The Brigham" as it is known in Boston, attracts patients and staff from all over New England, the country, and indeed, the world. The result is a fascinating scene as a stew of humanity moves each day as if in time-lapse through the great maw of the hospital's revolving doors. We learned from the information desk that our first stop was Admissions, and that it would be open for hours still. Reassured that there was no urgency, we migrated to seats on the lobby's sidelines. Picking up on Kathy's reluctance, I said, "So, no rush to go to Admissions, right?"

"She shrugged. "Hey, I'm going to be locked up in this place for a long time. I'm in *no* hurry to turn myself in." It was never spoken aloud, but I knew she had to be silently asking the question any patient facing the risks she was facing might ask: *And who knows if I'm even going to make it out of here?*

So, we sat a while more, then strolled around, finding the cafeteria at the top of the lobby's staircase and the chapel behind the information desk, exploring what would become our world for the next several weeks. Kathy and I lingered in the gift shop, each of us I'm sure only wishing it were larger, the better to occupy more time. We landed of course in the Au Bon Pain café off the lobby, for tea and cookies. Only after all this deferring and delaying did Kathy finally signal, "OK. Let's go see Admissions and get this thing going."

The unit that houses the Bone Marrow Transplant program is located on the sixth floor of a massive tower that looms over the main building on Boston's world-renowned Longwood hospital corridor. The admission process culminated in the first of what would be hundreds of elevator trips to "Tower Six" as it was announced each time the elevator doors opened to our new destination.

More waiting followed, this time in the Family Room outside the Transplant Unit. Like such rooms in hospitals everywhere, the small space was furnished with institutional decorator chairs chosen more for their cheery prints than for comfort, and presided over by a wall-mounted TV, which was on 24/7.

After a short wait, we were approached by a nurse with cropped carrot-colored hair who introduced herself as Toni Dubeau. She explained that she would be Kathy's primary nurse throughout the transplant. Like Kathy, she appeared to be in her mid-forties. A tall, attractive woman, she had a grin that instantly set us at ease and was totally Kathy's match in the arena of quick-witted banter. She would, in the coming weeks, live up to her flame-colored hair, proving to be a human comet of a caretaker, quick, smart, passionate, and funny. She would also come to feel like family.

Toni walked us through a brief tour of the unit. First, the doors. Huge, heavy, stainless steel barriers, they were automatic, to decrease skin—and therefore pathogen—contact and marked with foreboding signs: *No Admittance. Call if you seek entry and you will be buzzed in.* Clearly, portals to some other world.

Inside the imposing doors, the impression was of a superbly functioning spacecraft. All Times-Square-brilliant fluorescent lighting and stainless-steel surfaces, the unit was built so that each patient had his or her own cubicle, arranged in a pod-like oval around the central nursing station. As patients going through BMT must live for a time with virtually no immune system, the primary feature of the unit is that it is a sterile environment, a "boy in the bubble" kind of place.

We were shown where the filtered air was pumped in and directed to the washing station outside Kathy's cubicle, where we were instructed in the ways of unit hygiene. This involved long hand-washing with warm water, followed by the donning of yellow paper gowns, gloves, and masks. There were to be no balloons and no flowers or plants of any kind. No precaution was left to chance.

Then Toni slipped Kathy away to admit her to the unit, and promised to let us rejoin her shortly. When we did, Kathy was still in her own clothes, the only sign of any change in her status a plastic hospital ID bracelet. As a surprise, Toni let us know that she had paged Dr. Lee and gotten the okay for Kathy to have a pass to go out to dinner, as Kathy, still into delay tactics, had requested.

Pleased with the reprieve, Kathy, Greg, Tony, and I headed out to yet another favorite Italian place, in nearby Somerville. An unlikely word-of-mouth favorite, it was a hidden treasure. You entered through a Doritos-and-Oreos-type convenience store to find a tiny dining room in the back that served up huge helpings of wonderful food.

The mood was quietly festive, as if we had skipped out on school or work to grab this unanticipated treat. Kathy ordered a beer and ate bits of her pasta dish. Still nervous, she was buoyed by having at least gotten the long-dreaded admission over.

"I am so glad to have that nurse," she told us, clearly relieved as she turned her attention to the dessert menu. "She seems like a firecracker." We couldn't begin to know then just how glad we would all be to have "that nurse."

She got through two bites of her tiramisu, then, after lingering as long as we could, we returned to the hospital, where we dawdled some more, with the nursing staff as full accomplices. We crashed in the Family Room until late evening, to watch Tara Lipinski take the gold medal for women's figure skating in the Winter Olympics. Then it was reality time.

We kissed Kathy goodnight and watched with our hearts in our throats as the night nurse walked her into the day-light-bright unit, those great metal doors clanging shut behind them.

The first few days were quiet, almost anti-climactic after the anxious lead-up to admission. The quiet, however, belied the insidious task at hand. For the first step in the last chance that is BMT, oddly called "conditioning," involves exposing the patient to the highest survivable levels of radiation, in order to maximize the chances of killing off cancer cells throughout the body. In the case of non-Hodgkin's lymphoma, a component of the immune system itself is cancerous, so the lymphatic cancer and its metastases are the target of the radiation onslaught.

The radiation dosage is so strong that "it's as if she had been present at Hiroshima," Toni told me one afternoon as we rushed Kathy down to the basement-level radiology department. The trip down from the unit each day was tense. Since the radiation was doing its job of annihilating Kathy's immune system, Toni had to do all she could to hurry her wheelchair through the halls, calling dibs on the service elevator, and, as the doors opened on each floor, steering any newcomers away from joining us on the trip down, all in service of minimizing Kathy's exposure to the stew of pathogens that circulate in any city hospital.

Following several days of this brief yet potentially deadly

treatment, all appeared relatively quiet. It would take days for the symptoms of radiation sickness to appear.

With the radiation treatment, Kathy's body was now "conditioned," or prepared for the long-awaited transplant to take place. The actual procedure was far simpler than the word "transplant" implies. There is no surgical intervention involved, as in the more well-known heart or lung transplant. Instead, like in a blood transfusion, a bag is hung on an IV pole and introduced through a line in the patient's arm. Once inserted, it drips the bone marrow slowly into the body, where it is carried by the venous system to the site where it belongs. The whole thing takes maybe two hours. Then the real waiting begins.

The wait, which can take from 14 to 30 days, involves watching for signals that the new marrow is "taking" and beginning to produce its own new blood cells, a process called engraftment. During this time, the medical staff is watching vigilantly for early warning signs of problems that would signal that the transplant is not taking and the bone marrow is being rejected by the body.

Around 7 p.m. on February 28, 1998, on what in the transplant world is referred to as the patient's "new birthday," Kathy's bag of donor marrow was hung in her dim cubicle. At that moment, all we knew about the donor was that he was a 33-year-old man. If and when Kathy might wish to know more about her donor or contact him, she could do so only after a year had passed. This policy protects the donor from the emotional roller coaster that can immediately follow a transplant, and allows the patient to achieve some measure of stability and "new life" post-transplant.

Marrow donation is no walk in the park. It is a surgical procedure in which marrow is extracted via needle from the pelvic bone. It is done under anesthesia and requires some recovery time. We were grateful to the unknown donor, and Kathy was hoping to have contact with him one day to thank him, yet we were all keenly aware that a non-family donor was not the ideal option for her.

Later, I found a slip of paper with notes I'd jotted down the evening of the transplant. "George Clooney" I had written, since Kathy was speculating over why his ER character had been missing from the show for a few weeks. Pacing the halls later, as she dozed, a poem came to me.

The Mystery Donor

Life came stumbling back in
after the marrow drip,
so anticlimactic
on that midwinter evening.
The delicate young doctor enters.
In her hands,
cradled like a baby animal,
a plastic pouch

A pouch of rescue,
red red, so very red.
She and the nurse chant numbers to each other,

seemingly endless numbers
to ensure that this 46-year-old woman
receives these sacred cells
from this 33-year-old man,
matched as perfectly as possible
to bring her new life.

Already, jokes have been flying,
speculation raging
 about the identity of the mystery donor,
and which vibrant specimen of manly splendor
it might be.
They can't tell us, but we know, she and I.
She sussed it out and we giggle.

Dr. Doug has been missing for a bit
from his duties in the ER.
Kathy has noticed.
George Clooney will be looking a little pale, she says,
when he returns to the show.
But wasn't that so nice of him to do that for me?
What a guy.
I'm gonna have really cute bone marrow.
I know you can't tell me who it is,
she winks at her doctor,
but I've figured it out.
And that is some really cute bone marrow.
—February, 1998

Transplant Land

By day five of the transplant, we were under sail. It was not easy, but so far it was not unbearable. I called the unit in the morning and heard that things were relatively calm. Kathy had awakened briefly then gone back to sleep. At home, there was a flurry of e-mails and phone calls from anxious friends and family I needed to respond to before going back to the hospital. We had it arranged so that, at least during the day, she was almost never alone. But she was so eager when we arrived, I was sure she felt as if she was always alone. And of course, ultimately, she was. Knowing how important our presence was, I struggled with balancing the pull to be at her bedside and the need to manage things outside the hospital, finding, as I had all along, that there was no peace in any of my attempts. "Balance" was a mirage.

When Greg was with Kathy, I grabbed some quiet time at home. I did some yoga to move and stretch, meditated, and continued to walk in the woods near our house. It was a tremendous boon that we lived so close to the Brigham. Depending on traffic, we were as little as twenty minutes away.

The time passed in a surreal blur. Over the next several days, Kathy developed the anticipated full-on radiation illness. We huddled with Toni, who told us that she was in the critical part of transplant now, "where the miserableness becomes exponential." The symptoms of radiation sickness—diarrhea, nausea, mouth and throat sores—were all, Toni assured us, "normal, expected" parts of the transplant. They were simply the outcome of such massive radiation dosing. Now we were waiting for the white blood cells, the cavalry showing up on the horizon to show that help was on the way. But there was no sign of them yet. I found myself holding onto both hope and terror.

Kathy spiked a fever—another "frequent occurrence." They increased her antibiotics, and of course, medication for the discomfort: oxycodone.

Once the transplant was under way, the process became more fatiguing and challenging for all of us than we could ever have imagined. Some of the difficulty had to do with the obvious, external impediments. It was a struggle to stay present in the small, hot cubicle, gowned and gloved, and I felt frustrated by the mask. It was stiflingly hot, but more than that, it felt like it created a barrier between us. I felt kept from her somehow.

But these were small things not worth mentioning beside what she was enduring. That was what was increasingly unbearable. It was so strange. We brought in a relatively energetic, healthy-appearing Kathy, then watched as the treatment felled her. We watched her getting more ill by the day, not less. Her skin, reddened from the radiation sickness, was blotchy and puffy. Her eyes were glassy, and her hair began to fall out again. On her hands, shadows appeared, dark and bruise-like. She became unsteady on her feet. They kept reassuring us that these were "expectable changes, not dangerous."

My notebook became a place for me to sort out the overwhelming events I was witnessing on the unit, and the increasingly terrifying emotions we were all juggling. Here is an entry from that week:

Journal: March 9, 1998

These last few days, the full brunt of the danger Kathy is in has become very apparent. Her neighbor in the next cubicle is on a respirator and looks to be fighting for her life. Another patient died last week. I worked at not letting my alarm show as I watched the woman, who looked to be in her late 40s and had a husband who stood beside her rubbing her hands or staring, but never crying, slip away. I can't get the image of them out of my head. I'm so glad Kathy couldn't see and is oblivious to what is going on in the cubes right beside her.

It takes me back to what Kathy went through last year, and the promise she extracted from Greg and me about no respirator ever again. I pray to God the need never arises. Much of what I've witnessed has unfolded during the weekdays when I am here, and I've little heart to share it with anyone. Speaking about it—the mortal danger—makes it more real. I do talk with Tony, and he has been here with me and has seen it. He knows. And I've shared some with friends. But when Greg and the boys come on the weekend, I say nothing about what I have seen. Greg already sounded so frightened the other day on the phone, his voice so light and far away.

In her air-filtered cubicle, Kathy is insulated from outside challenges, both physical and emotional. All her life force is going into her own battle. So, when we arrive, regardless of what we've seen or heard on the way in, we work to smile, to greet her with tenderness and not fear.

From the hospital, I drive over to the studio, just to be. There, the only sounds are the heat coming up and the creaks in the old wood floor. I go there thinking I'll write. Instead, I make a nest for myself on the old sofa and fall asleep.

Lifelines

Kathy's room faced a concrete wall, without so much as a scrap of sky to remind her of the natural world. There was not a single source of beauty or visual relief available to her. Plants and flowers are not compatible with humans lacking immune systems, so they were *non grata* on the unit. The place was noisy, illuminated 24/7 with stark fluorescent lighting, and the food in the cafeteria made me wonder whether the pizza and burger bars were there to drum up business for the cardiac unit.

Once patients are admitted for transplant, there is no leaving the unit. This was their entire world. I wondered to myself about the designers of this environment which was meant to foster healing. What were they thinking? I knew of course that this was a super-intensive care unit, a life-and-death unit. But at times, for distraction from the ever-present anxiety, I found myself mentally re-designing whatever space I happened to be in. I thought of it as "redecorating mind," another form of therapeutic escape.

Needless to say, the hospital offered endless opportunities for this particular pastime. I designed rooftop retreats in my head, where, immune systems or no, there were trees and flowering shrubs in abundance, and soft chaise lounges with quilts for napping beneath a great blue canopy of sky. There was music off in the corner, a live cellist or piano player. And pets: kitties to snuggle with and a few lovely dogs to place their faces in your lap and just breathe with you.

Unlike Kathy and the other patients, I was able to step

outside, to find my own respite from this difficult environment. A stroll to the elevator and down to the lobby, which at midday resembled Grand Central Station at rush hour, could deliver me to the silence of the chapel. From the revolving front doors, it was a quick walk to a museum café in the neighborhood. There were still pay phones then, a whole bank of them were located off a hallway in back of the Brigham chapel. Literal lifelines in the time before cellphones took over, I used them to make countless calls to family and friends. I shared the up news of the day, or the down, sought support, asked for prayers, and gleaned news from "regular life outside" to bring back to Kathy.

Along with all of these external lifelines, there were the internal ones as well. My notebook and writing became a godsend during those days, if for no other reason than to offload the randomness and the worry. I would later forget how much I depended on pen and paper, though at the time it was a major coping tool: part containment, part digesting, part distraction. But in journal pages like these, found years later, I recognized how much writing had helped me to handle the stress.

Journal: March 11, 1998

The little notebook I'd bought for the express purpose of being able to write at the hospital has gone the way of my lists. It gets lost in my bag and becomes invisible. So, I wind up collecting scraps to jot things on—envelopes, menus, whatever is right at hand in the middle of things. At first, I thought I would just "make notes," then take them home and "really write." Hah.

I realize now that my scribbled notes are it. These and the journal pages, dashed off in the early morning. Because when I am over there with Kathy, writing is the furthest thing from my mind, the far-away unreal thing. I am pulled up against that bed, with her, as sentinel, nursemaid, clown, girlfriend, advocate, whatever the moment calls for. I'm talking or not talking, fetching things, calling Greg, and intercepting nurses or the endless stream of MDs to ask hundreds of questions. She, and her battle to live, is the only important thing, the only real thing.

But now and then, while Kathy is sleeping, I gather my scraps of paper and sneak off to the chapel, first to bow my head in the welcome silence, and then to quietly beg. We are swimming in such enormous currents in this place, in the waters of the ultimate mystery. And thankfully, I turn within to find faith more deeply seeded in me than I had realized, though not dancing to the music of the institutional church. Like so many who have been deeply disillusioned and angered by that body, my habit has been to hold it at arm's length. Yet in a strata beneath all the static, I find this green, living source, find that when I am asking please, please, please, somehow I believe I am being heard. That there is Love, listening.

And then, I scribble, on whatever I have. Guer-

rilla writing. Just to process it all. There is no one to talk to who understands what is going on over here, except ourselves—and Greg and I are talking constantly. We're all just putting one foot in front of the other, trying to do the best we can, navigating terrain we never dreamed of finding ourselves in.

The BMT unit social worker has asked a couple of times about our attending the family support group she holds on Tuesday nights. We've avoided it.

Greg, here every single weekend, is back home with his boys on weeknights. And as for myself? Avoidance, plain and simple. Once I got into that place and saw what was going on—that some people were dying in the cubicles around her—I knew I needed to stay away. I felt like I couldn't let in what was going on for other families. This was already hard enough. Funny to realize as a social worker that I am a 'resistant' patient!

When the social worker asks, I feel like of course I 'should' go. I tell her, "I know, I know," because I get the recommendation on one level. And yet, on a gut level, my survival level, I find myself saying, "Maybe next week." And then, I don't go. I go back and sit with my sister, and that's where I feel best.

So, there it is. I guess my journal pages, my stolen moments in the chapel, my scribbled scraps of paper, and my art studio buddies who listened to me read them *were* my support group, my lifelines.

The Siege

By St. Patrick's Day, Kathy was in a place of terrible struggle, with an infection in her blood as well as pneumonia. She was in desperate need of those new white blood cells (WBCs) to fight off the infections. She was so ill that Toni was assigned to Kathy as her only patient. She had a desk and chair stationed right at the entrance to Kathy's cubicle and was virtually never more than five feet from her, constantly monitoring her vital signs and blood oxygen levels.

We continued to watch her blood counts for some sign, any sign that the transplant had taken, and that her body's defense system was starting to stagger to its feet to make some WBCs. Helpless to do anything but wait, yet out of my mind with anxiety, I prayed constantly. "Please God, please, a shower of them. A shower of white blood cells. Even better, a blizzard."

I heard back inside my heart: *She will never be forsaken. Shall not. Ever. Be forsaken.*

But this was not exactly the kind of reassurance I was praying for. It sounded more like one of those "God answers all prayers, even if it isn't the answer you were hoping for" kinds of assurances. And that was not at all sufficient to placate me. "I want my sister. I want the boys to have their mother. PLEASE."

When I was home, Greg would call from the hospital, reporting on the day. We watched the blood work, waiting for the rescue forces. When would they arrive?

But then, instead of a respite, terrible changes began to take place, and she seemed to travel somewhere very far away.

Journal: March 19, 1998

My sister does not recognize me. Her eyes are glassy and unfocused, staring with directness, but with no spark of recognition. I speak to her, touching her through her johnnie. Her shoulder is a little knob of bone under my palm. She stares back past my head as I speak to her. She looks past me as if she cannot hear, out over my shoulder. Then I say something about how awful this is, and for a second, her eyes lock on mine and roll, speaking an exclamation as she nods her head imperceptibly. As if there aren't any words. And there aren't.

She sits straight up in bed, gripping her leg under her knee, and stares at the blankets as if they are confusing. When we speak to her, there isn't the slightest response. She goes on staring at the folds in the blankets, as if they are trying to tell her something, and occasionally turns to fix her gaze above our shoulders or on our faces, without any semblance of connection. It feels as if she's gone someplace and it takes too much effort, or it isn't safe, to come back. As if every meg of energy in her being is rushing on red alert inward to her core where a battle rages, leaving nothing with which to make contact with the world outside.

Toni bends over her, coaxing her, calling her "Kathleen," then, over and over, "Sweetheart," as she probes Kathy's ear for her temperature, arranges her arm for her blood pressure, grasps her wrist tenderly to listen for that driving, racing heartbeat.

Toni steps back, her face registering her concern. Kathy's mouth falls open. She stares and breathes, working, pulling in each breath. Large blisters bloom in her mouth, like blossoms left behind by the radiation, which blasted out the old house in order to make way for the new. Twenty days ago tonight, the new marrow hung in the spot where I sit, a simple IV bag on a pole, dripping the wine-colored marrow, and the chance for new life, into her body. After it was over that evening, she had been subdued, as if reserving judgment, until she passed through what would lie ahead. Until she passed through this.

An Anniversary and a Miracle

A sudden snowstorm swept in, mirroring the struggle going on in Kathy's room. Winds gusted and howled, hurling shards of hail and icy snowflakes in sparkling currents against the windows. Then, just as quickly as it started, the squall ceased, leaving only the winds behind. It was drearier without the snow, some magic was missing from the swirling air, now just bending the trees and making the house cold.

Greg and the boys had gone to Boston early to be with Kathy, so I had stayed behind. With the house empty, I sat in our room in the old rocker that Greg refinished for me years ago, as a joke.

Growing up in our shared bedroom, I was Oscar the slob to Kathy's neatnik Felix, and this old rocker was where I tossed my clothes until they fell off. It was the bane of her existence. When I married the first time, Greg refinished the old oak rocker, and he and Kathy had presented it to us as a wedding gift.

"Here. You get to mess up your own room now!"

So here I sat, in the faithful old rocker. Outside, the gusts of wind filled the air with a soft roar, a sound like the sea, without the predictable rhythm of ebb and flow. Black branches and twigs became filigree against the delicate new whiteness. It was a March afternoon to be inside, protected from the elements.

I thought of my sister, lying in her hospital bed, being

visited by her three beloveds, their pain and their love all entwined. When they came home later, their faces would be changed, their voices subdued. When I asked how the visit went, they would answer in monosyllables. "Oh fine," or, "Okay." And then we would be quiet, making dinner and huddling close. So much of this passage was beyond words. Kathy's mute vigil the last two days. Two teenaged sons, witnessing their mother withered to her frail, reedy essence, and a doting husband and father, helpless to change it. And me, anxious nearly to panic when I was away from her bedside, centered and focused only when I was there.

The next afternoon, a Sunday, I was sitting with Kathy in her cubicle when she suddenly returned from wherever it was she'd gone. After three days of non-responsiveness, she turned to me, and in a voice that was barely audible, said, "Oh, hi."

It was like one of those miracle moments in the movies. Every cell in my body wanted to cry out with joy, but instead, I found myself matching her quietness, fearing that if I startled her, like a doe, she would bolt and be gone again.

But she was back. Her eyes were still glassy—they would never truly be clear again—but she was back. She wanted to know if she could have a freeze pop. *Banana, please*. And was Greg here? And who had won the ball game? As if she had just dozed off for a nap. I called for Toni. We were ecstatic.

Toni told her, "You can have all the banana pops your

little heart wants! Hell, I'll drive to the ice cream store and fetch you a *banana split* if that's what you want!"

Kathy just smiled at our enthusiasm. She didn't remember a thing. "The drugs," Toni told me. One of the drugs they use during BMT, Versed, she told me, helps patients to not remember.

"They should dose it out to the family, too!" Toni and I cracked to each other simultaneously.

Frantic with relief, I dialed up Greg and the boys, who had just gotten back home in North Adams for Patrick and Liam's school week to begin.

"You won't believe it!" I tell them. "She's awake!"

She got on the phone with them, matter-of-fact as you please, slightly bemused by everyone's reaction. She asked about the boys' schools and sports and then about the Red Sox scores. I beamed watching her, beside myself with thankfulness. Into the bargain, oh merciful Lord, Toni told us that it looked from her blood work as if her WBCs were finally starting to climb. It was only a smidge, "an uptick" Toni called it. But, in the direction of up.

Finally, it looked like we might be on our way out of the darkness. I couldn't stop smiling at her. Kathy, noting the level of our excitement, reacted.

"Boy, I must have been pretty bad for you guys to be so happy," she told us. Toni and I filled her in a bit, Toni telling her, "Kathleen, you had us scared there for a few days. We couldn't get you to sass us back no matter what we did!"

"Sorry, I didn't mean to scare you." Kathy answered tenderly. As if she could have helped it.

No sorry. NO SORRY! Only welcome back. And lots of e-mails and phone calls to make, to spread the good news.

While Toni was busy with Kathy, I took a walk in the hospital to stretch my legs. Like so many of my walks, this one landed me back in the chapel, a sanctuary in this bustling hospital. A sanctuary for family members like me, out of their minds with fear or—like today—with thanksgiving, to have a place to come and get on their knees and lower their heads and say one of two prayers: *Please. Please. PLEASE.* Or: *Thank you. Thank you. THANK YOU.*

My frequent visits to the chapel had me redesigning that space, as well. A hospital chapel, I thought, ought to have long benches for lying down. Family members are already prostrate with fear and fatigue. It seemed like just the thing: a little lie-down while you pray. And maybe a mural of some inspirational sort, or a skylight or stained-glass window in the roof for staring. That would be just the ticket. If I ever got to leave the Brigham a big pot of money, I decided, that's what I'd do with it.

The quiet made space for another poem to arrive.

Psalm III
In the Garden

Down into the Quiet Place she went,
deep and far, where looks couldn't kill
and no stone turned.

She never asked, she never said she was going.
And we didn't know where to find her,
or if she would come back, or if there was some way
we could take up some of her burden,
and carry her
over the sharp places
where she could not step.

We watched and waited,
grave and tender,
touched her feet
through gloved hands,
anointed her small skull
with warm cloths.
When there was no sign
that she could feel our fingers
or hear our voices,
coaxing her back.

For days it went on like this.
We grew hopeful
when she opened her eyes,
only to have her stare out
past our voices,
over our shoulders,
back into the space.
(Was it dark or was it light?
Did she look with fear or with longing?)
Mute,

panting,
grasping each breath, then
collapsing back, eyes closed,
returning to her free fall.

Keeping vigil, we knew afresh
the scene in the Garden,
Jesus begging His friends:
"Could you not watch and wait with me one night?"
As He undertook His agony.

We held her hands
and said her name
and soothed her in her ear,
calling her Sweetie and Honey,
reminding her
over and over
of her name,
speaking the names of her sons to her,
like prayers.

And on the afternoon
of the third day,
yes, a Sunday,
she gathered herself,
bloody-kneed and dazed,
grasped the tether
which fastens her heart
to ours

and pulled herself back.

She asked for banana popsicles
and who was in first place.
She asked to use the phone.

She picked up the threads
that she had set down
and returned once more
to the time
of living-not-knowing.
—*March, 1999*

Spring, 1998

Preparing for Re-Entry

After 53 days in the surreal pod of Tower Six, Kathy's basic vital signs had stabilized—just barely—and all negotiating angles with the insurance company for more time had been exhausted.

The slog through the transplant process had been longer and harder than anyone could have prepared us for. Harder no doubt because of how ill Kathy had been during the respiratory crisis of the previous fall and because she didn't have a family donor. We had barely caught our breath from the stress of her recent comatose state when she was given a discharge date. We were all a bit stunned.

Like the transplant before it, the discharge process was fraught with challenges. A nurse from one of the home care agencies appeared in Kathy's cube one day, bearing a clipboard and a no-nonsense demeanor. She launched into a discussion about the discharge plan, which, to my astonishment, involved teaching me to perform the various procedures Kathy would need done each night after she came home from the cancer center. These involved giving her a number of injections and administering an array of other medicines, then flushing the IV port near her collarbone. She was being discharged with a total of 19 different doses of medication.

As the nurse began to elaborate matter-of-factly on how, after three days of nursing services to "get us up and running," Kathy would be discharged from VNA services and

I would take over her nightly care, the room began to spin. What followed was basically a meltdown on my part.

It went something like this: "I'm sorry, I can't ... No, no, you're not listening to me, I *can't*." I somehow found the presence of mind to take the nurse outside the room for what followed.

"I'm too tired, too wired, too frazzled to take on all of this! This is Kathy's survival involved here," I said. "What are you *talking* about when you say I can learn to do it? I can barely remember my way home some days, and you want me to take her life in my hands in this frame of mind?!"

I could hardly believe they would initiate this conversation in front of their patient, but apparently, they so take for granted the family's acquiescence that it would never occur to them to do it privately. In any case, this is when I hit my wall.

"NO. No, no, and NO. No way," was my answer. "I cannot. I don't trust myself and you shouldn't trust me either. If, out of fatigue and overwhelm, I make a mistake ... after everything she's already been through ... just, NO."

My meltdown was not well received by the agency nurse, who went off to pow-wow with the discharge team. It was obvious that they were taken aback, and clear that this shook up the plan. The plan being to discharge a critically ill patient with virtually zero immune system and ravaged by two months of radiation illness and a recent coma to an already exhausted family member who would also be driving her to the hospital each day and staying with her throughout the eight-hour stints of daily follow-up care at Dana-Farber. They would throw said family member a bone of two or three skilled nursing visits to get her started, and then pull out, leaving her in charge of the patient's medications, maintenance procedures, and keeping up the necessary immaculate living environment.

So cost effective. If I weren't a social worker, if I didn't feel the cost-cutting motivation coming at me like a locomotive, would I have been able to say no so fiercely? Is the average family member simply rolled over by the process? I don't know. I only know the "no" that came out of me was a howl that blew the very assertive intake nurse back several paces. Which resulted in our having a very nice nurse come to the house each evening from then on, to monitor and tend to Kathy's evening care.

As upset as I was about the situation, what felt most horrible to me was that any part of this conversation took place in front of the most vulnerable person—Kathy. Later, embarrassed, I went back in to apologize. She was her usual kind, funny self. She looked worried at first, which broke my heart. She told me that she was worried about me, and about Greg, and was relieved I had pushed back.

"I totally understand! What do they think families are made of?! I'd hate it if you two had to do more than you're doing already. Besides," she cracked, "believe me, I'd be fried too, if I were in your shoes. And I don't want *anyone* coming near me with any syringes if they're fried!!"

We had all looked forward to closing the transplant unit chapter Kathy had been living. Yet the notion of bringing home this pale, weakened version of her, with an obliterated immune system only just beginning to throw up tender new shoots was sobering on several fronts.

In the hospital Kathy's care, her very life, depended on the expertise of the staff and the impeccability of the environment. And in what is essentially an immune system transplant, the sterile nature of the unit is part of what sustains the patient's survival. Duplicating that care and taking her, frail as she was, out of that protective bubble was a daunting prospect, to say the least.

We poured over the Xeroxed instruction sheets from the hospital, which detailed the need to clean and disinfect everything with bleach and water, even prescribing the specific furniture polish to use to ensure that no dust went undusted.

Over the next two weeks, our Arlington home was scrubbed top to bottom by Greg and Tony and me, along with dear friends who came from North Adams to help. We took everything apart, cleaned it and put it all back together. All the blinds in the house, every lick of woodwork, all the upholstery and curtains, even the books. We groaned to realize that later, when Kathy was ready to return to her own home, we would need to repeat the whole process again in North Adams. But we got it done. If a house can sparkle as if Snow White's team of forest animals had swooped in and worked their magic, ours did.

Next, three large Styrofoam containers of medications were delivered, along with not one, but two auxiliary refrigerators to hold them. The refrigerators took up residence in our front hall. All this was just to hold her evening medications, as her daytime meds would be given at Dana-Farber.

Discharge day finally arrived.

I drove in to pick her up and spent the morning trying to conceal my dismay and worry as we dressed her, and I saw how unbelievably ill she still looked. Somehow, this became even more apparent once she donned her own clothes than it had been while she was in her hospital johnnie and flat in bed. I pulled the car up close to the entrance, and, together, her women warriors Dr. Lee and Toni wheeled her down to the hospital entrance to hug her goodbye. I snapped a photo of the three of them and caught my breath as I clicked the shutter. Above the hospital mask she would need to wear for months in public, Kathy's eyes were glassy and flat, the smile they tried to signal, anemic and forced for the occasion.

I felt as nervous as a first-time parent driving home a newborn. A very frail newborn. The car door slammed. I looked out past Kathy in my passenger seat to see the two beloved women whose expertise had brought us through the crucible of the transplant standing on the sidewalk waving goodbye, and it suddenly felt like some horrible joke that they were sending her home. I thought to myself that any-one as sick as she was at that moment could probably go right around to the Brigham ER door, be evaluated, and admitted to the ICU, STAT. But after nearly two months of the most intensive care possible, it was time to leave the safe-ty of the unit. Greg and Tony and I were on deck from that point forward. The aftercare plan, to begin the following day, reflected how vulnerable she remained: she was sent home to sleep at our house, with daily outpatient care from 8 to 5 at Dana-Farber, followed by nightly nursing visits.

That evening, the visiting nurse came for an hours-long intake and inventory of the medications that filled both newly installed refrigerators. She administered Kathy's evening meds and flushed her port, so that for the first time in eight weeks, she could sleep in a setting that said *home*.

Nervous as we were, we eagerly organized around the new treatment routine. Even with all the schlepping it would entail, the intensity of the aftercare plan felt welcome. We were relieved that they would continue to follow her so closely. And, even with our anxiety, comforted to have her finally back home with us.

Springtime

Kathy had spent 53 days in a noisy stainless-steel and fluorescent-lit cubicle, her sole window facing a cinderblock wall. Driving her home from the hospital, I yielded to an instinct to divert our route to stop by the pond near our house. I pulled up close to the water, sparkling on the soft April morning, the air chill but blazingly sunny. I switched off the motor and opened the windows and we sat in silence. Bundled up in a winter parka and fleece cap, with a blanket across her lap, Kathy's face behind the surgical mask was paler than the clouds overhead. We were still for a long moment, and I could feel her drinking in the scene before her, as if pulling in sweet, cool water after a long drought. She sat without moving or speaking, taking in this sustenance, so long denied, which the natural world offers us every single moment, today's offering made in its sublimely beautiful April clothes.

Early spring was just breaking out. The pond, newly thawed, reflected the optimistic blue sky, the trees in various stages of budding, the very air moist and bright after the filtered air of the hospital room. I sat beside her and felt her encounter with this fairly typical spring moment unfold as if for the very first time. Felt her stunned to silence like one who'd been dwelling in a cave or inside a blindfold all these weeks, and therefore receiving the world, feeling it, being acted upon by it, as if receiving a sacrament. Ducklings glided past us. Young mothers rearranged squirming toddlers in their strollers. The sky beat down on us its steady sunny blue.

We sat and sat. I didn't even glance at her, only stared ahead, not wishing to impose myself on this private reunion she was having with the world. Moments passed that felt eternal. Was it ten minutes, or sixty? Neither of us broke the silence. We only sat and stared, the awe in her stillness so palpable that I too, was enveloped in it.

As battered as she was by what she had just been through, getting the chance to visit with the ducklings, the shoots, the pale beauty of early spring made me hope that, just like the new growth exploding around us, she would only gain from here, growing stronger from that morning on. And go on for years, hopefully to experience enough onsets of spring to perhaps even fall back into taking them for granted once more.

As it turned out, that isn't what happened. And because of that, I find myself visited now and again by moments that feel of a piece with that one at the pond. On a fine spring morning a question will suddenly cross my mind: *I wonder how many more Aprils I have?* A question that surely could seem morbid if dwelt on for too long is not so scary when administered in gentle, even homeopathic doses. A question that can bring forth a different me, a less distracted, more present me. And suddenly I am back there, at Kathy's pond-side reunion with the sky and the plants and the birds, thanking the evergreens, blessing the sky, breathing in the budding leaves.

I'm sure there is a Rumi poem about this very thing, or maybe forty of them. *Our time here is short: wake up, wake up!* But those poems? They're about Rumi's moments. And Rumi wasn't there with us that morning by Spy Pond. This was Kathy's moment. And through her wordless response, it became mine, too.

Easter Sunday brought welcome spring-blue skies and gentle temperatures. Honoring Kathy's love of holidays, we planned a traditional ham dinner and figured out Mass times. While Greg and Tony hid eggs and prepped vegetables, I walked Kathy, attached to a rolling IV the VNA nurse had started that morning, to the shower.

She shook her head, sighing with appreciation for the sensory pleasure of warm water against her skin.

"Most days Toni did sponge baths with me. I think she went through a hundred facecloths for every bath. She'd swipe it over me once, then toss it on the floor and take a fresh one. We won't use so many of your facecloths here, I promise!" she told me.

We had gotten a shower seat so she could sit, which she did, turning her face into the warm water. When I motioned to hand her a towel, she waved me away. "Not yet, just give me a few minutes more," she said. When she felt finished, I bundled her into one of our fluffiest towels, helped her into new blue flowered flannel pajamas and a cap, and wrapped her up in a warm robe.

"Can you take me outdoors for a little while? The air felt so good the other day by the pond. I just want to be outdoors again for a little bit, with the kids."

Greg and the boys, still elated to have her "sprung" and home for her first holiday, set a chair of honor in the shade where she could watch Patrick and Liam hunt for their Easter eggs. At their age, the egg hunt was done more out of tradition and to amuse their mother. In high spirits they wrestled and yelped, putting on a comic show of brotherly competition, bringing the hoped-for laughter. Very shortly our neighbor, who couldn't see the adults seated beneath her, came to her second-floor window to shake her finger and call out to the boys, chiding them.

"Don't be fooling around out there! Don't you be getting too close to my lilies, you'll trample them!" She stood in the window and glared down. Patrick and Liam looked up at her in confusion before turning in unison to survey her untrampled but alluring orange daylilies. Of course, Tony and Greg had nestled some of the eggs into the extremely large and robust lily patch, and their bright colors beckoned from amidst the flowers.

Tony quickly interceded on their behalf. "It's all right, Becca, I hid a few Easter eggs for them. They'll be super careful." The eggs were found, and we chuckled at dinner over how Easter eggs had suddenly become a problem.

"Well, sometimes when people's worlds get very small, even little problems seem like big ones," Mom interpreted for her grandsons. At our dinner table, it seemed the opposite was unfolding. It was the littlest things, the warm shower, the fresh warm clothes, the dinner table festive with flowers and lined with people we loved, and even the normalcy of a cranky neighbor, that all seemed so satisfying and precious.

As I went through the day I found one of the prayers from the offertory of the Mass playing on a loop inside my head: *In Your mercy and love, keep us sheltered from sin and pro-*

tect us from all anxiety, as we wait in joyful hope for the coming of our Savior.

As we wait in joyful hope.

Those were the words that kept singing in my ear. After the thousands of times I'd heard that offertory prayer at Mass—as a girl in Latin and later in English—that phrase kept rising up in me and humming through my blood. It was a stretch, from where we were, but I found my mind repeating those words over and over like a soundtrack, a mantra for the time we were living. As we wait in joyful hope.

That afternoon as Kathy napped, another poem arrived.

Psalm IV
Easter Sunday

I did not go to church this Easter,
a fine, perfect dream of an Easter morn,
Cloudless blue and streaming sun
enveloping our house and calling us out.
We marveled at the day and smiled,
counting ourselves already blessed.

I walked my sister, one step by one step,
to the shower,
our Easter Parade.
Watched her face soften,
a smile of welcome and relief
as the warm water washed her clean.
She leaned her head against the tiles,

sat a long time in her shower chair,
and basked.
Then we rubbed her down with oil,
and dressed her in her flowered PJs
the blue flannel ones with lace,
a small cotton cap, her Easter bonnet.

We made our way, pushing the IV pole,
back to the bed to rest from our excursion.
Later we went outside,
where she perched in a chair,
and watched her boys searching for Easter eggs,
clowning and performing,
to make their mother laugh.

She turned her face into the sun
and once again we saw that small smile
of receiving life,
which was our Easter service:
her life force resurrected,
and rising up
to have a little dance
while her body rested
in the light.

This was my Mass, this Easter morn:
to sit in the presence of one
who has gone down into the darkness
and rolled away the stone

and returned,
definitely the worse for wear,
yet transformed, transfigured,
in ways we cannot yet see.

To sit in the presence of sheer courage,
pure heart,
to witness her spirit reach
and stumble back toward life,
her ravaged body fueled by love and grace.

This will be my worship service this Easter morn,
as I set the table and bake the ham,
each moment a prayer of thanksgiving.
—April, 1998

Grace Street

We had prepared the guest room for Kathy to sleep in, but she landed most nights on our sofa. The living room was spacious and bright, with oak floors and lace curtains framing tall bay windows that looked out onto a riot of spring rhododendrons. Still adjusting to life outside the hospital, she craved sunlight and claimed the triple-steam-cleaned-but-rumpled sofa, so she could wake to the sun pouring in and the purple blooms peeking through the windows as if to visit with her.

"I'm very comfy here!" she assured us, as she tucked in for the night. "I couldn't have any sun or flowers in the hospital, but this way, when I wake up, I have all the sunshine and flowers I want right outside my window!"

For myself, I loved waking up and tip-toeing around the kitchen, stealing glances at her in the next room. Still asleep, her small flower-capped head poked up from beneath a patchwork quilt faded from repeated laundering. I loved having her back. I embraced the sense of hope—that sense that we were in a new phase, one where we would help her to rebuild, and truly heal.

Our new routine meant waking early each morning and, after getting some tea and, if we were lucky, an egg into her, heading back to Dana-Farber. Given her immune status, she had to continue wearing a mask whenever we went out. Once at Dana-Farber, she was usually given a private room for the day's schedule of IVs, medications, blood work, and frequent small meals supplemented by intravenous nutrition. Dr. Lee would be in and out. It was clear that they remained quite concerned about her. Except for sleeping at home, she may as well have still been in the hospital. But the continuity was reassuring and helped us to adjust to life outside the transplant unit.

They were very long days. We got home at 6 or 7 p.m., at which point the visiting nurse would arrive for yet another hour of evening care. Kathy's nutritional status was so important, but it always felt like we were squeezing in dinner.

Four days after the start of her new day hospital routine, when we were all about ready to drop from fatigue, we got a call from our Dad's nursing home to let us know that he had come down with a virus that was making the rounds there. Then, just as Mom was preparing to head back to be with him, we got another call letting us know that he had died peacefully, with one of my cousins and the parish priest, an old friend, by his side.

Before heading out to western Mass for the services, I went for a long walk in the park called Menotomy Rocks, around the corner from our home. A little wooded patch right near the city, its lovely pond reflected light in every season, and its hillsides, studded with rock outcroppings, felt as if the Native Americans hadn't left so very long ago. It had become a refuge for all of us since the outset of Kathy's illness, a place to walk and think, or walk and cry as was the case that day.

It was almost impossible to grasp the reality of my father's death, given what we were living. Already deeply exhausted, I was stunned by the news and for a while, I was frozen. At any other moment in our family life we would all have been at his bedside. When we were children, my mother and our aunts had not been squeamish about bringing us into the sickroom or to the deathbed or wake of an aging family member. We had been shown how to just be there, to touch and soothe and keep vigil together.

Dad, 1980.

I had been particularly close to my dad as a child, his buddy. His warmth and truly unconditional love, regardless of whatever struggles he was enduring, had been a lifelong gift. While he had been more and more absent as his dementia progressed, he was still capable of lighting up when we entered the room to visit and welcoming us with smiles and traces of his dry humor. Well into my fifties, he would sometimes use the nickname he had called me as a kid, winking and remarking, "I can't get over how tall you're getting, Big Red!" The news that he was suddenly gone felt surreal. But it required an immediate response and planning. How would we manage the intensity of Kathy's care in Boston and take care of a wake and funeral in the Berkshires?

I found my way to a great boulder high on a hill, well off the walking trail, where I sat, trying to let my Dad's passing sink in, with only the rustle of the leaves breaking the silence. In the shelter of the trees and the rocks, something in my chest opened and I was able to weep. I was soon joined by a very concerned golden retriever, who had wandered from his master and galloped up the hill like a dog on a mission to take his place beside me with his head in my lap. I had never seen this dog before, yet here he was, finding me in my hiding place as if bent on comforting me. He stayed for a few long minutes, alternately burrowing his head into my chest, licking my face, and watching me with his great brown eyes. When he heard his owner call out "Ripple! Ripple, come!" he snuggled and snuffled at me once more, before bounding back down the hill, his parting yelps sounding like a lament.

It was an amazing moment, a moment that felt oddly divine. I couldn't help thinking about my Dad, who had died within the last two hours, and his love of animals and of dogs in particular. What was that little visit all about? I didn't know, but I returned from my walk with a lifted heart and shared the story of my warm doggie comforter.

We buried my dad in a beautiful Berkshire cemetery enveloped by the hills, remembering him in all his lanky handsomeness and his ever-present Irish wool caps. We remembered his warm wit and his helplessness in the face of any animal who needed shelter and feeding. In his later years, he had become a one-man Help Line, making dozens of phone calls each week to people who lived alone, people who had now joined us in the circle around his gravesite. Given his dementia, he had never known what Kathy was going through. And it was just as well.

While we were away for Dad's funeral, Greg stayed behind in Boston to care for Kathy. During those few days, she was readmitted to the Brigham with a cough. When we returned we found her back in Tower Six, but in a regular hospital room separate from the transplant unit. After all the time she had spent there, it felt odd, like going to stay in the house next door to your house. And she didn't have Toni to nurse her; her caretakers were all new.

To further complicate things, because she was coughing and there was a question that it might be tuberculosis, she was quarantined. To our horror, we found the nursing staff covered up, not only in the familiar yellow paper gowns and gloves, but adding a new head apparatus that resembled a Lucite version of Darth Vader's helmet in *Star Wars*. Picture Darth Vader in buttercup yellow. I watched as a new nurse checked her IV, and while I appreciated how gently he leaned in to explain what he was doing, still, I could only imagine how frightening this guy—who looked more like he belonged on a hazmat team than at a bedside—must have looked to her.

Yet again, Kathy drew on her time-tested tools to cope. She caught his name from the white board on the wall and made eye contact.

"So, hey Gary, nice headgear. You look like you could diffuse some landmines for me while you're in here."

We saw Gary's shoulders shake slightly as he chuckled and the two of them were off, relating human to human, paraphernalia or no.

We also had to don the yellow paper dresses and the face-masks that we had worn early on in her transplant. It was hot, it was cumbersome, and it was scary. We were all very doubtful that she actually had TB, so we felt rebellious and slipped the masks down to kiss her forehead. Once again, we watched and learned; if Kathy could face the setback without falling apart, then certainly we could face it too.

Watching her navigate this new challenge, I flashed on a memory of chatting with Kathy at the sink one afternoon, as she washed and I dried. "How are you coping with all this?" I had asked. "What's helping you?"

She had fixed me with her Kathy gaze, intense, taking things head on.

"Faith," she had answered. "I don't talk about it a lot but I'm actually quite religious. I don't always get to Mass but I do pray."

We talked a bit about my own raggedy path of leaving the church and pursuing decades of yoga and meditation. I was still trying to find my way spiritually, but could no longer deny how deeply the faith of our forebears was seeded in me. These last months I had hounded the heavens with Hail Marys, and found surprising comfort in meandering over to the noontime Masses near my work.

"Well, we come by it honestly. We are Mildred and Colbert's children, after all!" I laughed.

"And I'm glad we have it," Kathy said. "I hope one day the boys will find their own way, that they'll have something to hang onto when these hard things happen, or to give thanks to when the good things do."

So, while we had both drifted from the intense loyalty our parents had to the Catholic church, and though we hadn't discussed it in a long time, in our proverbial time of need, we were both turning back toward the faith of our ancestors, a faith which felt like a pure thing, apart from what we both viewed as the problematic monolith of the institutional church. Now, as she reminded me of her belief being part of her daily life, it made sense. As we watched her face wave after wave of hardship, we were witnessing her faith, alive and shining through her quiet strength.

There were times when, in the face of her courage, I felt rushes of, for lack of a better word, guilt. Guilt that she was enduring this ordeal, while I was free to leave. Free to head home or to make forays out into the world. Sometimes, during her hospital stay that spring, I would slip out for an hour to have supper, trying to time it while she was napping. On one exquisite evening, I took a walk to the Museum of Fine Arts cafe, to sit and stare at the list of phone calls that needed to be returned while I drank my tea and waited for my salad. It was a refuge of beauty close to the bustling hospital neighborhood, where I could sit with some soothing music in my headphones, a display of the museum's beautiful cards and prints in the nearby gift store window, and a brisk fifteen-minute walk pulsing through my blood.

I thought, as I often did during our family's siege, of the preciousness of these places of quiet and beauty in our mad, mad world, especially in times of pain. Places that offer solace and reprieve, through art, nature, or simple beauty, whatever the suffering of the day is. Long live museums. Long live chapels and churches. And while we're at it, remembering those first hours on admission day, long live hospital gift shops.

I'd promised Kathy I'd be back soon, so I stayed only for a quick bite, just long enough to feel the museum around me—a change of scene from the hospital. But, as always when I left her, I felt torn. She was used to having me there during the week, when Greg was home with the kids, and they could be lonely, scary hours. There were calls I needed to make, things I needed to take care of, but I hated to disappoint her. She asked for so little. So yes, I felt some guilt in being able to walk away from the hospital to sit in a beautiful spot and enjoy some lovely food, yet continued to find it important to renew myself so that I had something to "bring back" to her.

It turned out that indeed there was no TB, and the head-gear disappeared. Yet another course of antibiotics took up residence on the IV pole beside her, and Kathy began, once again, to recover. Once she started to stabilize and her coughing diminished, plans began for another discharge. We were eager to get her "home" once more to Gray St.

My body, however, decided to not cooperate. Suddenly, I was sick, taken over by flu-like symptoms. It was terrible timing. I felt like I could sleep the day away, yet there was major housecleaning to do if we were going to safeguard her newborn immune system. The housecleaners we had hired to help had called at the last minute to cancel, also citing illness.

Siblings: Kevin, Kathy & Maureen, 1983.

But help was on the way. Just when we needed them, Greg and my brother Kevin arrived from North Adams. Kevin had flown out for Dad's funeral from his home in Washington state, and was staying on for a couple of weeks to help Mom settle after Dad's death, and to help with Kathy's care. It was an indescribable solace to have him here. His sheer presence felt fortifying. He made me laugh, and he happily pitched in to cook. We came home from the Brigham one night, famished, to find him hovering over a stovetop bubbling and splatting away, with our family comfort food, pasta and meat sauce with warm garlic bread, all ready to serve.

So suddenly, the sounds of Kevin, Greg, and Tony, the Three Amigos making each other laugh, filled the house. Watching Greg sitting at the table nursing a beer and chuckling as he razzed Kevin, I could see the comfort his brothers-in-law brought him. And for myself, I felt stronger and more grounded just knowing they were there.

As the men hustled to get the cleaning underway, I napped and ate the good food they cooked and got better. Once again, we made plans to bring Kathy home in a few days.

Our house was full and, circumstances notwithstanding, I loved having everyone under one roof—my tribe. The meals, the banter, the comforting under-footness of it all was a kind of sustenance. Our home had become a refuge, and the sprawling one-floor layout provided privacy and quiet back in the sleeping spaces, even when the kitchen and living room were hopping.

Amid all the worry then, there was also palpable gratitude for my family and having a home where we could gather and make our way through this time together. I had begun to think of our Gray Street home as Grace Street.

Sherpas and Icy Marbles

Another date was set for Kathy to come home from the hospital, but once again, it had to be delayed. Now Tony, who was never sick, was feeling flu-ish. Dr. Lee, saying "better safe than sorry," decided to hold off for another day.

But maybe it wasn't quite sickness. Having just come through my father's death and funeral, we were all exhausted. Kevin was still visiting, so one afternoon while Tony napped, he and I went out to buy groceries and some badly needed tires for my car. Then we headed home for naps and Vitamin C.

I remembered to take the shopping list with me—that at least was progress. Yet even when I took my list out, I found that I had trouble seeing it. It was as if I didn't have my glasses on. Those days, when I was out in the world, it felt like life outside of bone-marrow-transplant-world wasn't quite real, as if it was shimmering or waffling. I couldn't quite get it into sharp focus. It was "normal" life, not the hospital and the fierce struggle happening there, that seemed like the dream.

Finally, after all the setbacks, came a leap forward. After just a few more days of follow-up at Dana-Farber, Kathy was cleared to go home to North Adams. Elated, Greg and their western Mass friends scrambled to get their house cleaned and ready. We helped Kathy pack up her few belongings from our guestroom, and I could feel her practically vibrating with excitement and eagerness to get on the road.

"I can't believe it!" she said. "It's been nine weeks! I never dreamed it would be this long. It will feel *so* good to be HOME!"

We stood waving at the top of our sunny driveway as she and Greg backed down the hill honking happily, then turned away onto the road home.

That night, I caught the feeling of the day in my journal.

Journal: April 29, 1998

Kathy is home! On the one hand, I can't help reflecting on how HARD, how bloody awful, how rough it's all been on her. Yet, as Toni had promised, Kathy doesn't seem to remember, at least not the worst of it. And tonight, she is back in her own kitchen with her family. That will be its own powerful tonic for her. She still can't go out to socialize, so there will be no gatherings with the hometown girlfriends just yet. Her doctors continue to keep vigil over those white blood cells. But sluggish as they were out of the starting gate, still, they seem to have staggered to their feet and started their forward march. Alleluia.

So, bone-tired though we were, there was also this lightening, this feeling that finally the worst of the battle was behind us. That Kathy had come through her transplant.

After the relief and celebration of Kathy's discharge home, Tony and I got to spend some time on Cape Cod. A former high-school classmate of Kathy's had a B&B there and had generously invited us to come for a few days to decompress.

When I spoke with her, she told me, "We recently had a close call with our own son. We are so grateful for his recovery and the help we received that we wanted to do the same for someone else. And when we heard about your care of Kathy, we knew we wanted to offer you what we could—a getaway."

They could not know what the peace and beauty of their offer meant to us. A place to rest and to walk a bit and process all that had happened, including Dad's death, which had seemed so surreal in the midst of the events swirling all around us. I nearly wept with gratitude when we got to the Cape and closed the door to our lovely room. We both needed hours of sleep and quiet.

At first my mind raced, reckoning with the intensity of the past few months, and the changes I knew were coming right around the corner. I hadn't used my full FMLA leave, but after nine weeks, I had made arrangements to return to work. I knew the job would be challenging once I got there, so my sense of overwhelm had come along on our getaway.

And quiet, quiet in all its forms, seemed to be the antidote. It let me step away from the storm of details in my head, to gaze up at the great pines wafting against the springtime-blue sky, and to sit on the cool sand and stare out at the sea, alive with light. The Cape is quiet off-season, so we had the beach pretty much to ourselves. Time to just hold hands and walk and talk about all that had happened. Later, we threw down a blanket and curled up in the sun for no talking, just soaking in the beauty or napping. All of it was so good for us, like relationship vitamins.

As we relaxed, the memories came, images and memory fragments from the last few months, surfacing as we stared at the sea or walked. As if we were only now, off the juggernaut of the transplant and hospital stay, able to let them in, like snowflakes swirling in eddies, and settling at our feet.

I realized that I had no idea how to "get ready" to return to work. The foster parents we worked with at the agency were amazing people, and I was happy to be part of the team that provided training and support for them. And the kids, for the most part, were resilient survivors who really benefitted from all of the "extras" that our well-funded agency provided.

Nevertheless, the day-to-day work involved a good amount of adolescent acting-out and family conflict. So, as I contemplated returning after months of almost constant personal crisis, I wasn't at all sure I had the reserves of adrenaline that were often needed. Yet, with my savings exhausted, not returning was a choice I didn't have the luxury of making. I took notice of my reservations, but shelved them during our holiday, deciding to deal with them later.

One early morning, walking on the beach, I was flooded with memories of Kathy's transplant nurse, Toni, who had become like a third sister. With her eight- to twelve-hour shifts, Toni had been our guide, caretaker, teacher, and companion. Who could begin to name what she had done for Kathy?

The nurses on a transplant unit have a lot in common

with the sherpas who accompany climbers ascending Mount Everest, except that their charges are making the climb while deathly ill with radiation sickness and the other ailments their downed immune systems are at risk for. Like any relationship forged on an epic journey, the true intimacy was between Kathy and her nurse. But Greg and I had bonded with Toni as well, each in our own way. She had become our interpreter, educator, coach, and fixer. She was as direct and fearless as if someone's life depended on it—because it did.

Toni always called Kathy by her full name, Kathleen. She was the only person who did so, and it was one sign of their special relationship. One morning before Kathy left the unit, Toni had pulled me aside to tell me, "Listen, Kathleen may live a long time, or she may not have a long time. Her body was pretty beat up when she came to us. So, I told her to suck up every day. Not to wait to do things. If there are things she wants to do, to go watch Liam play basketball or Patrick play soccer, or other things she wants, she should do them and not postpone them."

Clearly, as difficult as it was for me to hear those words and absorb their meaning, she wanted to let us how very fragile Kathy remained. After all that had transpired, I wanted to put an "on the mend" sign up and move forward with caution. But then I'd flash on Toni's words, and, difficult as they were to hear, I felt grateful that she was brave enough to say them.

The news at that time was full of headlines about Linda McCartney's death after her bout with breast cancer. She too had had a bone marrow transplant, at Memorial Sloan Kettering Cancer Center in New York. The news of her death was a cold clutch in my chest, a reminder of what can happen even further down the road from discharge. I flashed on the suffering her family must have endured, losing her after all they had been through, and I thought about Patrick and Liam and Greg. Amid the relief of seeing Kathy home at last, the what-ifs, made vivid by the headlines, rekindled the dormant fear that sat like an icy black marble, heavy in my heart.

Then, as had happened so often, just when we could use some form of uplift, an unexpected opportunity occurred. We learned that the Dalai Lama was making a one-day appearance at nearby Brandeis University, and we jumped at the chance to see him. Tony was deeply immersed in studying Buddhist teachings, which for me, too, had become yet another lifeline.

The occasion was a wet, wild, and windy May day, and we found all the inconveniences predicted: lousy weather, a long hike from the nearest parking lot, crowds and waiting lines everywhere. But it was a lesson in priorities—all those things fell away within the larger sense of our good fortune at the opportunity to be there, rain, lines, and all. The pervasive feeling of the crowd was cheerful acceptance of these minor inconveniences as a small price to pay for the chance to participate in the event. It was remarkable to see this enormous crowd, so orderly and—yes, peaceful—just melting at the sight of His Holiness. There was a felt-sense of being in the very presence of love, and from the crowd: love answering.

The Dalai Lama emanates, radiates love and something else: a deep good humor. As he passed by, his warm, twinkling face nodding in greeting, a wave of giggles went through the crowd, as if he'd sent off sparks of joy that were infectious. After all the grief and loss he has been through, he truly appears to embody what he teaches. "My religion is kindness," he says. That's a religion I can sign on for. Soaking rain, waiting lines and all, we felt blessed by the day.

Momentous Occasions

It was a time of recovery, all around. I had returned to my job in early May, so I was back working with my rambunctious teenagers in foster care. As summer came around, Tony and I went on a meditation retreat at the Insight Meditation Center in Barre, Massachusetts, with some teachers we both liked very much. Several days in silence would not be everyone's notion of fun. Yet for us, the stillness and the sitting in the big house with the great trees all around it felt like just the thing. More time to let our minds and our bodies go quiet and settle with all that we'd been living.

Back home, I continued to sit and meditate, and to make my prayers in many different voices, from the conversational to the frantic. The Thank You prayer was currently high on my playlist. Kathy was home. I could call her up and we could resume our chats, dissecting and laughing at our lives. Though we could only begin to understand how coming through the last months had changed both of us.

For myself, I felt that the ordeal had knocked some edges off, had humbled and slowed me down in ways that felt welcome. I remembered the time after Megan's passing, when the loss was still a gnawing pain in my chest, while at the same time I felt a new appreciation for the smallest kindness coming my way. I remembered spending one afternoon with my then mother-in-law at the stove. She was busily cooking a chicken and simmering filling for a lemon pie, because she was worried that I was losing weight. I had been so moved watching her, and so filled with gratitude that all these years later I could still touch it.

Like the friends who hosted us at the Cape, I remember promising myself, *I want to do this for other people. I don't want to forget this feeling of how someone's kindness has touched me.* I had felt knocked over by sorrow then, while at the same time keenly, vibratingly alive. As crushed as my heart felt, it also felt broken open, the very rawness making me more able to be moved. Yet, however much we might wish to hold onto the intensity of such aliveness—albeit without the sorrow—we mostly can't. It tends to fade, as it did back then, as we are pulled back into the mundaneness of our daily routines. So, as difficult as these last months had been, I was back in that place of deep gratitude once again, and glad of it.

In transplant time, the days out from BMT day are counted carefully. Each day out from the "new birthday" is a sign of the transplanted immune system "taking," beginning to function on its own, with less and less bolstering needed from the blood bank and the pharmacy. By early May, Kathy and I figured out that she was fast approaching day 75, and that June 7th would be her 100-day marker, a huge milestone in the transplant world.

She seemed to be doing amazingly well. Since she had begun to make enough platelets of her own, she had stopped needing regular transfusions. Even after all the waiting for the platelet surge, it seemed incredible to all of us when it happened. In a way, the further out from the transplant we got, the more remarkable it all seemed. It was the opposite of the toothache that you poke with your tongue to test the pain; instead, an inner stream of relief was so palpable that I kept returning to touch it. And marveled, every time.

After a year of classroom study, Tony had finally begun his clinical internship, which meant putting into practice all that he had been learning, providing hands-on treatment to patients at the New England School of Acupuncture Clinic. With that too, we were entering a new stage, leaving behind the remarkable, rich, awful, and it would seem, miraculous, months of Bone Marrow Transplant, and heading into a time when he would begin, finally, to practice his new profession.

The wonderful news was that he loved it. He was completely fascinated by the workings of the human body and how this beautiful thousands-of-years-old medicine acted upon it. He loved getting to know and help people, and he continued to soak up learning in his field like a thirsty sponge, with enthusiasm and passion. It was a marked shift for him from the high-stakes, high-anxiety world of the contracting business, which he'd been in for twenty years, and one that I felt would add years to his life.

Kathy and Greg came back to Arlington to stay with us for her weekly check-ups with Dr. Lee. One evening, following the two-and-a-half-hour drive from North Adams, she sat in our kitchen looking absolutely perky, not needing to immediately lie down and nap as she had after past trips. It was a high summer evening, the house still bright at 7 pm. I had prepared comfort food, so even with the wide windows flung open, the kitchen was filled with the smells of garlic and to-matoes, garden herbs for the salad dressing, and warm bread resting on the counter. Instead of racing off to get into her pajamas for bed, Kathy eagerly pulled up a chair at the table.

"Oh, thank God you cooked! We didn't want to stop on the way and now I'm starving. Pass me a chunk of that garlic bread, would you?"

Greg cracked open a cold beer for each of us, and we all sat down to tuck into supper. Watching Kathy eat a little spaghetti, just like old times, I felt a rush of joy fluttering in my chest. Instead of jumping up to squeeze her, as was my impulse, I simply sat beaming at her across the steaming plates of pasta.

To further my amazement, I made going-to-bed noises before Kathy did. We were in the living room catching up after dinner and she was thoroughly enjoying herself.

"So Tony, how is your student clinic going?" she asked. "Were you afraid when you had your first patient? I mean the first time you try to put those needles in someone new, I'd be a nervous wreck."

Tony assured her that he'd had so much practice work-ing on fellow students during his training that he had felt on pretty solid ground. During the first year of her illness, when she might have benefitted from acupuncture treatment to help with the side effects of chemotherapy, he had only be-gun his training, so he hadn't been in a position to offer her this care. But now he was.

"You're wanting to be sure you're on the right point, that's important, but I'm not really afraid about doing it, no. If you want a treatment sometime, Kath, say the word. It could help you with discomfort or side effects, or even with the stress."

Kathy was open to the idea. "Sure, if I get side effects again, I'll tell you. I have so many appointments as it is, I think I'm good to stay with Dr. Spector and my Dana-Farber treatments for now. But if you see a place for it, let me know!"

I was loving the visiting time and reluctant to let go of the evening, but with my recent return to work, I was bushed. I was back to making home visits and attending appointments and meetings. While my kids and their foster families had been happy to see me again, and kind in their concern, we were quickly off and running with the focus on their challenges, as if I had never left, which was just as it should be. I headed off to bed while Kathy, animated, stayed up chatting with Tony and Greg.

As I went to sleep, I thought about how Kathy had said she expected Dr. Lee to say she could come in less often, now that she was doing better. It brought up a funny reaction for me. As inconvenient as these trips had been for them, selfishly, I would miss seeing them reliably every Sunday evening. The four of us had become a tight unit, our worlds shrunken to center around Kathy's treatment and each other. It had been an enormous comfort to be in such closeness, but it was time to pick up the strands of our lives and move forward. So, for their sake I hoped they got that green light, another marker of her progress.

Love, Holding Us Up

Maureen and Tony, Summer, 1998.

My first job after college was teaching first grade at a Catholic school in the Berkshires. The other first grade teacher was a veteran Irish nun, who was the total package I so admired: a superb teacher as well as a wildly funny and mischievous human being. Now and again of an afternoon, she would send one of her kids to my desk with a note that read: "Ireland's free for the afternoon!"

At first I had no idea what her note meant, but I quickly learned that it was a reference to the then-British occupation of Northern Ireland and roughly translated meant that the authorities weren't around, or in this case, our principal was off to a meeting for the rest of the day. It was shorthand for "the boss is gone, let's take the kids outside to play!" Forever after, "Ireland's free" became part of my own lexicon, indicating the chance to cadge some unexpected play time.

One July afternoon, while we were still getting used to life's intensity being ratcheted down, I noticed that Tony and I were both restlessly circling the house. When I found myself opening and closing the refrigerator, looking for something that wasn't to be found there, I called out to him.

"Hey! Ireland's free for the afternoon, let's do something!" It didn't take long to decide to head in our favorite direction, to the north shore.

"You pack the car and I'll check the fridge to see what we've got for the cooler," I said.

Within half an hour we were heading north, with the local folk/acoustic radio station providing a cheerful soundtrack to the drive. We arrived around five and threw down our beach chairs. There are always at least a handful of people on this beloved beach, so we were not alone. We watched the gentle end-of-day promenade of strolling walkers, Frisbee throwers, and folks with their dogs playing at the water's edge. As we took in the scene and watched the rolling surf, all opal colors in the fading daylight, we each felt the welcome sensation of some space opening up in our chests. We munched on the Thai food leftovers we brought, fragrant with lemongrass and pineapple, and talked over the news that Kathy had indeed been cleared by Dr. Lee to move out her check-ups to once-a-month. Tony shared my slightly bittersweet feelings, since this meant they wouldn't be coming to Boston as often, but we shared a deep sense of relief as well.

"It's time. They need to recoup from all this too. Things will begin to settle down now," Tony said. "At least, let's hope so. There will still be the ups and downs, I'm guessing, but hopefully the worst is over."

We got up to walk the beach for a while, rolling up our jeans to wade into the surf still warm from the day's sun.

"I hate to leave the beach," I said. "but I'm still hungry! You?" Tony smiled as if to say, "You know me, I'm *always* hungry!" "How about we head over to Captain Vito's and get some fried shrimp?" he suggested.

We drove to our favorite Gloucester hole-in-the-wall and picked up some take-out, then headed back to the beach to grab the last rays of the day.

"I guess it's time to leave," I finally sighed. The light was nearly gone and the air was beginning to turn damp and chilly. We held hands walking back to the car, refreshed.

We were home by nine, but those few hours by the water felt like a mini-vacation. Staying open to these slivers of free time helped us sustain our energies for the longer haul, and to stay connected as a couple.

Then, toward mid-summer, a new problem developed. Kathy couldn't eat. She'd lost all of her appetite and interest in food. When she did get some food down, there was a new intestinal problem. She wasn't absorbing what little she was eating. What began as a time of relief turned into the Summer of Worry.

My mother, the 81-year-old former nurse, began making the ten-minute bus ride to Kathy's house several times a week to sit with her and try to coax an egg, a milkshake, some mashed potatoes—anything, into her most-precious patient. Tony and I had to restrain ourselves from calling hourly for feeding reports, an exercise in discouragement for all concerned. When Kathy's next Dana-Farber appointment came up, I found myself harboring, still, the hope that they would come up with some magic bullet, some deft solution to the worrying lack of appetite.

Dr. Lee prescribed capsules of Marinol or THC, the active ingredient in marijuana, to try to stimulate Kathy's appetite. When that didn't work, she prescribed a hugely expensive food supplement called Scandi Shakes. Up to this point, our interactions with the local pharmacist had been fairly painless. We dealt primarily with a young woman who, bless her heart, was as cheerful and earnestly helpful as the pharmacists in the TV ads.

But through this time, as the hospital tried anything they could think of, we sometimes found ourselves caught in a bitterly frustrating dynamic. We would leave Dana-Farber as quickly as possible and I'd drop Kathy off to rest at the house. Then I would dash to the pharmacy, desperate to fill the latest prescription and start getting the hopefully miraculous substance into her, only to find that the pharmacy did not have what we needed in stock, or the insurance would balk, giving some obtuse reason. We were grateful that Kathy and Greg's insurance had, for the most part, covered her extremely expensive care–including the supplement shakes–but given the urgency of her symptoms, even a temporary delay was enough to fuel our anxiety. More than once, I found myself standing at the pharmacy counter, encountering the obstacle *du jour* and thinking to myself, *I might just have a heart attack, myself, right here.*

With Kathy back home, we resumed our weekend caravans across the state, the twists and turns along Route 2 and the Mohawk Trail long since memorized. Our trips had become even more frequent, since we needed to keep a closer eye on how Mom was doing in the wake of my father's death. Tony's mother, in nearby Pittsfield, was also aging, so the need to "look in on the girls" took on more importance in our routine than it had in the past.

One Friday in late July, as we descended the hills into North Adams, Tony and I got into a snit of a fight. Even as it was happening, it seemed so foolish, but erupting out of the accumulated tension and worry, things quickly got heated. It was about Kathy's increasing failure to thrive, on top of renewed job pressures and assorted other stresses. We were both struggling to stay on our games at work while worrying about the new complications of Kathy's recovery.

But mostly it was about Kathy's eating. Or lack thereof.

Tony was irritated that her medical team hadn't come up with more. "Why aren't they treating her more aggressively? She *has* to eat! She can't live if she isn't eating!"

Reacting, I took the position of defending the team, too

frightened to acknowledge what he was implying—that they didn't know what else to do for her. "They're doing the best they can! What do you expect?!"

The argument took on a life of its own from there, so that we wound up on opposite sides, when what we both wanted was the same: Kathy eating and thriving.

We pulled the car over at the Hairpin Turn, a dramatic spot where Route 2 jackknifes and begins its descent into North Adams. Looking down at the little city of steeples encircled by rolling green mountains, we tried to talk things through and collect ourselves. But it was hard. We were both depleted, emotionally and physically. The best we could do was to put a patch over it like it was a bum tire and drive on.

Our visit was colored by this start, with both of us drained. I woke up in the middle of the night with a stab of anxiety in my chest. And once anxiety with its sidekick adrenaline reared its head, all sleeping bets were off. I got up to read. And on Sunday, I felt ill with fatigue, as did Kathy, who wasn't sleeping either. So, the much anticipated weekend of visiting with dear friends who were in town from Tucson to see Kathy wound up feeling more than a little disjointed.

As we reversed our route across the mountains, Tony and I made time to reconcile. We stopped along the Deerfield River at a curve where enormous boulders jut out into the water. It was a long-cherished spot that we called "Qi Rock." We clambered out onto the great boulder and sat facing the currents, feeling the elemental energy of the rolling waters settle us. In our trips across the state, we nearly always paused there to sit a while, receiving the blessing of the river, which was never more needed and appreciated than that afternoon.

Then we gave in to the impulse to take a detour. We turned off Route 2 and made our winding, climbing way up West Mountain Road to Stump Sprouts, where we had married just a year before. Lloyd, the owner, invited us to stay for dinner, so we sat at twilight on the slope of the mountain, eating vegetables newly picked from the garden and gazing out into the greens and dusky purples of the ancient hills. We breathed in the evening's gentle, tree-washed air, and remembered. The landscape, the food, and the warm welcome worked their alchemy and we left feeling restored.

The beauty of the western Massachusetts hills.

We were reminded of why we love western Massachusetts, its people and its land. Always a place of beauty and renewal, it gave us this healing day. And although the detour, in the midst of exhaustion and crammed schedules, didn't seem like it "made sense," once again, as had happened often along this hard path, following our instincts and doing the unexpected turned out to be exactly what we needed.

One evening shortly after our visit, Greg called to say that Kathy had been readmitted to Berkshire Medical Center and had had a seizure in the car on the way there. She was also having severe pain in her neck and shoulders and had recently fallen while walking in the yard with her friend Donna. All of this was added to the other dangerous problems around eating, weight loss, and dropping blood numbers. The medical team made plans to do a CAT scan and a spinal tap, followed by a bone marrow biopsy to assess what was going on. The feelings of dread returned. Even our prayers felt worn out.

Again, I struggled with what to do, how to help. Should I stay home, or head back to the Berkshires? My tortured decision-making process kicked in, with a weeklong conference ahead that I had committed to for work. And on the home front, time with Tony had become so scarce while he was in school that it was hard to leave. We were both tip-toeing on the top of the stress line, surfing it, somehow managing, but only just.

I decided not to head to the Berkshires but to go ahead with the work conference on the Cape, with Tony accompanying me for the trip. Ironically enough, the conference topic was Attention Deficit Disorder. Since I was the personification of distraction, my attention was *definitely* at a deficit. The only thing I could concentrate on, and in fact was laser-focused on, were the phone calls to western Mass. But none of the news was good, and no sooner had we arrived on the Cape than I regretted my decision. We were torn: do we pack up and leave? Both of us were obsessed with worry, and its cousin helplessness, about how Kathy was spiraling down.

I was haunted now by the nurse's words: "Kathleen may live a long time, or she may not. She was a very sick girl, coming to us." I was also asking myself: *Are we doing enough to help her and Greg and the boys?* Followed closely with: *What more might we be doing?* In such a situation, how much is enough? When someone you love is gravely ill, how do you rest? How do you ever feel you are doing "enough"?

In my clearer moments, I could recognize that my mind was racing around its tracks of What to Do Next in a reach for control, a series of desperate rescue fantasies. But this was not like the time I trashed the egg salad sandwich back in nursery school, when with a few deft moves I could right my little sister's world.

It was no longer a question of blocking out the possibility of losing my sister. We needed to open the door to that room now, to allow for this unthinkable other outcome. For months now, we had kept that door shut—firmly shut and locked. We had put up curtains and tried to carry on as if the other room, the "sunny" room, was the only room we lived in. The hopeful, it's-all-downhill-from-here, slow-but-steady room.

Now I found myself forced to cross the threshold of the darkened room, to turn on the lights and open the windows.

This was the room where it didn't end the way we wanted it to, where things didn't go our way. Yet we had to yield to this possibility, if it was beginning to unfold. Because otherwise, we left Kathy in the darkened room all alone, when the sole reason for her struggle was to have more time with her boys and all of us.

I breathed all of this in. Breathed in that I had to open that door and leave it open, and move some plants and tea-cups into that room, too. I had to let in all the possibilities. Because, of course, they were already here.

During the conference week at the Cape, Tony and I celebrated our first anniversary. We spent the day at the beach, ending in the silver-blue twilight. With the tide low and the stars just peeking out, we drew an anniversary card in the sand. Then, we had a candlelit but subdued dinner at a Wellfleet inn. Without forcing or planning in any way, we let it happen simply and quietly.

We wondered to ourselves over dinner: *What a first year of marriage!* Yet, however difficult it had been, how could I not feel grateful to have *us*, to be together in coping with it all? Tony was as involved, as fierce in his concern and love for Kathy as if she were his own sister. I felt a physical sense of balm when I was next to him. He pulled me in close and things felt more bearable. Then his eldest-brother, goofy self would emerge, clowning as he did so often, and get me giggling. However much our hearts were pierced by worry, there was also this: the sense of love holding us up. And so, gratitude.

Stolen Grace

Once again, Kathy stabilized sufficiently to be discharged home. And once again, we weren't exactly clear about what had caused her setback, nor what had helped her, except that steroids were usually involved. The biggest news was that the newly produced bone marrow was lymphoma-free. This was great to hear, but the marrow, we were told, remained "sluggish," and wasn't producing enough new cells. So, in addition to the steroids, they began once again administering those precious platelet bags.

The importance of this resource is so obvious, yet I had never given it much thought until someone I loved needed it. Since day one of her diagnosis, long before any transplant, Kathy's life had relied on transfusions of blood platelets donated by other human beings. The units she had received would be counted in the triple digits. It was deeply moving to learn that many people give blood regularly, as often as they can. Many of the donors are grateful former patients or family members wanting to give back for the help they have received. Talk about a circle of life.

One afternoon while Kathy was receiving her platelets, I tried to join the ranks of the donors. As has happened before, I was screened out as a donor because my blood pressure was too low. When I returned bearing two cups of tea, having failed in my mission, Kathy got a kick out of the news.

"God! If you don't have high blood pressure going through this with me, I guess you never will!" she said. "But how many people have to worry about their blood pressure being too *low*?!"

Very inconveniently during this summer, my support team began to jump ship, with my therapist moving to Texas and my acupuncturist going on maternity leave. Although both had helped me so much, I couldn't summon the energy to look for and start over with new helpers. I recalled with new humility the many times as a social worker I had encouraged others to begin again with a new provider, and how frequently, in the shifting field of health care, people are called on to make such changes.

My acupuncturist's advice before her leave was for me to continue to work on balance. I needed to balance "putting out" energy, both at work and with family, with restoring and replenishing. It was a nice thought. I got it. But in the day-to-day juggle, I had no idea how to do it, except to keep grabbing naps. As a result of all those surgeries back in my 20s, I had become an elite, Olympic-pedigree napper. Also, walking in nature, grabbing time with Tony or my girlfriends, and always, putting pen to paper at the studio or anywhere I could, helped. That's how I filled the prescription for balance—with moments of stolen grace. But when a crisis hit—and so much of life at this point felt like a crisis, "balance" seemed like a country I'd visited once but whose landscape I could scarcely remember.

Then one day, looking for some wisdom or grounding, I turned to the *I Ching*, an ancient Chinese system for accessing wisdom. The process involves throwing three coins six different times, making note of the pattern of heads and tails, then reading the "judgement" indicated by the coin patterns from a guidebook. I consulted not the classic Wilhelm and Baynes guidebook, but instead two beloved and well-worn books by women: Rowena Pattee and Carol Anthony. In my patchwork quilt of spirituality, I sometimes found the *I Ching* helped me access a new perspective or find an exit from whatever dark alley my mind had gotten trapped in. As usual, I was dumbfounded by how on-target the text felt.

My question had to do with how to do this balancing act, and the Anthony book turned up a reading titled "Standstill Changing into Contemplation," which counseled retreat and quiet. The words, as the Quakers would say, "spoke to my condition": "In times of darkness and difficulty, when we perceive no progress, tension and conflict can arise. The remedy is to disengage from looking at the situation until inner calm is restored."

Reading it, I felt a click of recognition in my body. The text advised me "not to get caught up in dreading the future or anticipating negative situations. Make a sincere effort to be resolute against fears." It was a good reminder to live in the present and not in some imaginary future I dreaded, and it gave me something to hold onto for the moment.

There was more relief when we got home and had a late-night phone call with Kathy. She was eating a little bit, oh kiss the ground! Wily nurse that she was, Mom had wondered if Kathy's anxiety about not being able to eat had taken on a life of its own and, testing her theory, had given Kathy half an Ativan. Then she presented her with one of her favorite foods, raisin-cinnamon bread pudding, baked in her special cobalt blue bread-pudding dish. Per Dr. Lee's orders, she was trying to increase Kathy's calorie intake, so she made the pudding rich with eggs and cream and maple syrup. Her mother's instinct was right on. Mom was encouraged by the day's success and was already looking for ways to build on it. Kathy sounded relieved as well, though she was more interested in telling me who was being laid off at the supermarket in town and checking on how Tony's acupuncture practice was going.

"I take each day as it comes," she told me as we wound our conversation down. "That's all I can do. So, today was a good one. Mom and I high-fived in the kitchen. When I can get a good day, I'll take it!"

She spoke for all of us. Once more, we slept well that night.

Taking Tea with the Mystery

Before we knew it, Kathy was back in the hospital, this time taken by ambulance to Berkshire Medical Center. She had fallen again, and Greg had come home to find her burning up with fever. While waiting for results of the blood work and cultures to track down the source of the fever, they had started IV antibiotics, along with TPN (nutrition via tube) and platelet transfusions.

Yet again she summoned her resilience. After the various infusions, she sounded more like herself on the phone, her voice stronger, some of her sass restored.

But so many questions remained unanswered. Why had her white blood cells, which had been on the rise, precipitously dropped? Why was her marrow "sluggish," the word they kept using to describe how slowly the new marrow was taking up its life-saving function? Despite the recent confirmation that the transplant had "worked," that indeed her marrow had been declared lymphoma-free, complications and side-effects that had been listed as risks in those early transplant consultations were now emerging. And because, as Toni had pointed out, Kathy had been a particularly frail candidate in the first place, these complications were bearing down hard on her, creating this jagged path of recovery.

Fear was the undertone to everything. In the last three weeks, she'd had a seizure, fallen twice, had a 103.8 fever, seen her white blood cells plummet, and had lost even more weight, getting down to 94 lbs. In spite of her appreciation for desserts, she had always had a very petite build. But you witness, when someone is very sick, how little margin a lean frame leaves for the ravages of illness.

Mom told me about one of her recent afternoons with Kathy. She'd been going to Kathy's a few times a week to help when the boys came home from school, and to ensure that, as much as possible, Kathy wasn't alone. They were having tea when they looked at each other across the table and both began weeping.

"She's really afraid that she's dying," Mom told me. "We had a terrible cry, both of us. It was about that, even though neither one of us could bring ourselves to say it."

There were moments like this on the journey, when the reality broke through. The reality of Kathy's death as a distinct possibility. That had been the unbearable "third rail" we had all avoided, the unthinkable, the unspeakable. Despite all the setbacks, all evidence to the contrary, we had pointed ourselves solely, fiercely, in the direction of fighting. Yet, some fights are lost, right?

When I looked back on this time, I wondered how it was for Kathy. Should we have initiated a conversation about this possibility more directly? In not doing so, were we taking our cues from her? Or were we protecting ourselves? And what sort of protection is that, anyway? While we were "sparing" one another from what was becoming more and more a real possibility, we were also isolating ourselves from one another, and thus missing out on all that might be shared, during one of life's deepest mysteries.

The image of the two frailest ones—Kathy and Mom—alone together at the dining room table facing down the unbearable made my heart hurt. And yet, frail perhaps on the physical plane, they were both ninja warriors of spirit.

Later I wondered why I hadn't followed up and mentioned this event when I talked next with Kathy. Why not make some reference that would re-open the door to it, and possibly provide another chance to move closer to her? But I didn't. Instead, I waited for a sign from her, and so the two of us continued our dance of avoidance.

Perhaps that was what she needed. Or maybe what I needed. It's a wondering that will never be answered, one of the koans from that chapter of our lives, a sliver of regret lodged in my heart.

The next hospitalization spiked anxiety into panic again. Once more, my every impulse was to hop in the car and head west. Yet the weekend ahead was the last one before Tony began his crazy-busy final year of training, and it was packed full with things that needed doing. Now my mind, like a NASCAR racer, began circling the track at 150 mph, spewing conflicting needs and anxieties.

Patrick was getting ready to leave for college. Did he need any last-minute shopping that Kathy couldn't do? Liam had seemed a little at loose ends on the phone lately. It had been ages since he'd insisted that I stay on the line while he cued up some grunge rock—Nirvana or Pearl Jam—for me to hear, then picked up the receiver to exclaim, "Okay! This is the Best Rock Band EVER, right?!"

We disagreed, of course, but I remembered how I had felt about the Beatles at his age, so I'd hold the phone away from my ear, listen to what sounded like screeching through my receiver, and smile.

It would be good to be of some comfort or use to both of them, and to Kathy and Greg. Could we get out there and cook something that might tempt her? Or clean? Laundry? Something? Anything?

All I knew was, my whole body, my every cell was saying to me: *My sister's time won't wait.* Too anxious to do anything else, I packed up my to-do list and Tony and I once more headed west on Route 2.

Back home the next week, late summer rains arrived, steady and soaking. How to prepare, I wondered again as that to-do list suddenly felt meaningless. I went to my quiet front room, lit a candle, and picked up my pen. Writing my way through my fear had helped me cope all through this time. So once again, I began.

Journal: August 25, 1998

> *They've run all their tests. They do not know why the spark is flickering, nor how to coax it back. This, with a team made up of the best medical minds and a family's deepest prayers. Within, I feel myself kneeling at the rim of the great mystery, head bowed. I breathe and pray. I make an offering of patience, of faith. I recall Steven Levine's teaching about "taking*

tea" with our demons or with that which we most
fear, befriending what we most want to avoid. I re-
member it and breathe. I claim a place in my chest,
loyal and pensive, for hope, and breathe through the
aching fear in my gut.

More time please, I find myself bargaining. My
heart feels heavy with this terrible sense of clarity
and calm. I wish I could just scramble away, or go
to sleep. The litany goes on beneath my heartbeats.
Please, please. Are you listening? Do you hear? Do
you care? Are you even there? I have to believe—
believe you are alive in each of us, breathing each
breath into being, infusing each cell with its next
pulse, drenching the very air, our hearts, her strug-
gle, all of it, with your Presence, with Your compan-
ionship. So that we too, are not left alone with this.

I talked with friends who asked how Kathy was and how
we were doing. I found myself spilling over about how panicked we were, watching her body fail. The floodgates opened,
and it all came pouring out of me. And I immediately felt it
was too much.

How much of the details and emotional intensity could
people take in? Some needed to back off, to veer away from
it, and I understood. If in our own family we had been reluctant to acknowledge what was happening, how could I blame
anyone else for being so?

I'd certainly been guilty of being skittish around other
people's tragedies. Several of our friends had walked this

road not long ago with older relations. How "there" was I, truly, for them? I remembered having fleeting moments of judgement of others at some points: Isn't she over-involved? Isn't it time for him to let go of this and move forward? God forgive me. What would we all do if that was how friends responded when illness or tragedy struck? If people all held us at arm's length, as if saying, "Oh this is too hard, too in-convenient. Let us know when it's over and your chipper, fun self is back!"

I guess that most of us are deeply afraid of this place, the living-near-the-borderland-of-death place. Yet our avoid-ance leaves us stranded in quite a lonely land when our turn for loss inevitably comes around.

The important thing to remember, of course, is the simplest. Most folks caring for a very ill loved one are over-whelmed and desperate for someplace to air it out. What helps is a simple "How are you today? How goes it?" Fol-lowed by simple listening. And, if welcomed, the ancient and equally simple hug. Not solving, or suggesting, or even com-miserating—just listening. Ironic, given my field, that I need-ed to remind myself that it makes a difference, just to listen.

During the Labor Day weekend, we planned to go to New Hampshire for the wedding of our friends, a weekend-long event at a camp where the bride had spent many summers. We looked forward to the joyous celebration, a chance to visit and dance with old friends. As we left to head north on Friday, the phone rang, and it was the bride asking us if we might stop at their house in Concord first, to fetch the wedding rings they'd left behind—a welcome moment of comic relief.

As we made the drive north, I stared at the trees starting to change into their early autumn colors and replayed much of what we had been living. With the space provided by the long drive, my mind also began wandering to questions about my work future. It seemed odd to be thinking about this in the middle of Kathy's illness, like entertaining some grand hypothetical theory during a fire. Yet there it was.

Traveling this road with Kathy had changed me and left me questioning how I was spending my life. I was feeling more and more pulled by something I couldn't quite see, something right out of the corner of my eye. I kept thinking about the oft-quoted question posed by poet Mary Oliver in her beloved poem, "The Summer Day," asking what you plan to do with "your one wild and precious life?"

A Pisser of a Heart

The more we saw up-close the limits of medical science when it came to treating late-stage cancer, the more I turned to help in realms beyond. Early on in Kathy's illness, I began dashing over to a chapel near my office in Lowell for the noontime Mass. I had discovered the small and very sweet St. Joseph the Worker Shrine, situated right across the street from the high school, during a lunchtime walk. I had come of age during a progressive time in the church. Pope John XXIII was throwing open the doors and windows to acknowledge the modern age. My high school and college heroes were the Jesuit war protesters Daniel and Phillip Berrigan, and artist Sister Corita Kent. As the church swung sharply more conservative, and therefore in my mind more merciless, over subsequent decades, it had disappointed, wounded, and infuriated me. But this, I could do.

I walked over to the chapel, a small, cool, dark space which always smelled like incense, and sat with the elderly, and the mothers with babies, and the worried-looking businessmen, and we bowed our heads while the organist, an ancient priest, rocked back and forth with his eyes closed, coaxing hymns out of the creaky organ. It became a part of my day that I found enormously comforting. I was almost always moved to tears at some point in the service, though of course, it didn't take much.

One day that fall, it was the sight of a heavyset man I

imagined was a teacher who had dashed over from the high school so quickly he hadn't stopped to put his jacket on, arriving late in rolled up shirtsleeves and loosened tie. He slipped into a pew, crossing himself quickly as he dropped to one knee and inclined his head toward the altar. As the priest droned on, his voice fading in and out on the outmoded sound system, the teacher knelt in bowed stillness, oblivious to his surroundings, a shock of white hair falling over his forehead, his hands held to his lips in prayer. A few long moments in the middle of his day, probably his only break, to visit with his God. Then, as if awakening, he lifted himself from his bent prayer and took his place in the familiar ritual.

The priest's words were largely inaudible, yet the text was so deeply embedded, so written on the heart, that those around me carried on aloud, reciting the old prayers along with him. It was a quick, somber Mass, full of people who looked, like me, as if they'd come here badly in need of help—nourishment at lunch for the struggling or frightened, comfort for those nearing life's end, a quiet place to bring life's deepest sorrows in the middle of an ordinary day.

The end of Mass had its own rhythms and rituals, especially here in this chapel, whose periphery was ringed with life-sized statues of Christ, Mary, and a greatest-hits gallery of saints, with rows of flickering candles in front of each. You dropped some coins into a box as an offering, then chose a candle to light with one of the long wax tapers, sending your prayers forth. A beautiful and mysterious practice, it awakened memories of lighting many a candle as a child with my parents.

I lit many candles for Kathy over those months, gravitating to Mary or St. Therese. As a little girl, someone had given me a picture book about St. Therese, also known as the Little Flower. I remembered her story. *Therese, you were one of four sisters, you would understand this sorrow.* At my mom's request, I lit candles to St. Anne, the mother of Mary and the patron saint of mothers. Around me, my fellow lunchtime pilgrims made their offerings, and said their silent and, I imagined, equally desperate prayers. I always lingered for those last few moments, in many ways my favorite part of the ritual.

How to reconcile this sense of comfort, of "home" and history and heroes in my church alongside the sadness and anger I have over the role this same church has played in quashing and constricting human life, human expression? The same church that maintains its (largely ignored) ban against birth control, consigns its homosexual or divorced and remarried members to roles as second-class citizens, and denies condoms to third world countries struggling with HIV? That forced a progressive priest out of politics, while hypocritically sticking its nose right into the halls of Congress—so much for separation of Church and State? That stubbornly denies women access to the full expression of their gifts as priests, based on the customs of two thousand years ago? And worst of all, whose bishops protected predator priests instead of the innocents they preyed upon, and have never faced any consequences?

The questions hang over my life, full time, unanswered.

At times, the Church as institution feels to me like your

boozy, perhaps dangerous old uncle. He's a blood relative, but you approach warily. While here, in the workmanlike little chapel near my office, it feels beloved to me, the church of my people.

Whether it was divine intervention or simply part of the struggle of her recovery, Kathy's health once again took an upward swing. She and I talked over Labor Day weekend, the air still warm enough for open windows, yet the scent of autumn already in the air. I had called to see how she was, and how plans were going for taking Patrick back to begin his sophomore year at college.

"Why don't you come?" she asked. "It'll be fun."

That was all I needed. On the face of it, given what I had on my own plate, my decision was a bit frenetic, yet as it unfolded, there was only a sense of peacefulness. My car could practically find its own way from Boston to the Berkshires, and as soon as I arrived, we loaded into their car for the next leg of the trip. Driving to New York State in the packed-up car, amid their friendly chatter, I was reminded again of what a tight, strong little family they were.

And the best part by far was that Kathy—hospitalized only weeks ago—was better. Once on the campus, she not only roamed the buildings with us, but repeatedly climbed the three flights of stairs in the dorm, lugging clothes, comforters, and pillows as she did. She walked across the campus to the student union with good cheer, as if she did this every day. Watching her, we were exhilarated. This rebound, coming in the wake of the summer she'd had, seemed like another unspeakable gift. Once again, we all thought: maybe. Finally.

Kathy showed every sign of wanting to move on from all the focus on her, all the special treatment. She just wanted to get on with life. On the drive home, she told me that she and Greg had recently "laid off" the team from their community, who had been taking turns cooking for them all these months. In protective mode, I raised some half-hearted objections, but she just shrugged, "We're good. We're fine. I told them to find someone else who needs cooking!"

It was a good day, a normal back-to-school trip for a boy and his family, with the focus on him, not her.

After kissing them all goodbye, I drove homeward at dusk along the winding Mohawk Trail, feeling filled up. There were campfires glowing along the Cold River, and further along, tipis circled a pasture where a Native American pow-wow was underway. I pulled the car off the road and opened my window to listen to the drums and take in the smell of the campfires as an orange moon rose full, casting its light over the Deerfield Valley. It felt as if, through some synchronicity, my full-hearted elation at seeing Kathy so like her old self was finding its perfect expression through the mystical elements of fire and drumming and moonlight. I drove on, lifted, smiling to myself.

A few days later I met Kathy in the lobby at Dana-Farber for one of her check-ups. An entry from that evening captures the optimism of the moment.

Journal: September 13, 1998

Strangely, despite some recently observed but undiagnosable "streaking" on her chest films and the seizure last month, it looks like Kathy is coming up whole again. How can this be? We watch and count the ways. Her skin looks healthier, her color better, her short hair thickens and curls. At the nape of her neck, a little tail appears.

I watch her from across the Dana-Farber lobby this week. By 10 a.m. the waiting area is already littered with spent coffee cups and tired-looking newspapers. As she walks down the hall for the 50th or the 100th time, there is an electricity about her, a hum of victory. She crosses the lobby toward me, this time without a mask, without holding onto anyone's arm, and only wavers once. I watch her approach and notice first the way she holds her head, high and determined. Stubborn. Feisty, even. Take that, you bastard cancer. Then I see glints of large, hoopy earrings. I will not look like a patient today, her look signals. No loose comfy sweatpants for her. Instead, she is Kathy—classic and tailored. A slim khaki skirt, royal blue cotton sweater, unfussy gold jewelry, makeup, and pumps. She catches my eye and smiles.

"How would you like to do my blood draw for me today?" she jokes. "My veins are crap. I'll go get our coffee and you go see the nice lab tech. Do we have a deal?"

A frail wraith of a woman, with a pisser of a heart, she is proud of herself today, emergent after these desperate months. Her slightly cocky grin conveys a silent message: No big fuss please. But for any of you who doubted, I was always out to win this.

In spite of the many downs, when these ups came, they were manna from heaven. We embraced them. We gloated over them. The relief was so physical and so immediate, it felt as if the concrete girder that had been living on my chest had been lifted away and the space had newly filled with light. She, of course, did her blood draw, and then met with Dr. Lee and the team, charming everyone as she went. Then, because her appetite had slowly begun to show itself again, we headed for the cafeteria to get down to the real nitty-gritty. What kind of desserts did they have today? Lemon pie? Chocolate pudding? Molasses cookies? We sighed with contentment as we slid into our booth, hot tea and sweets in hand, to have a slice of normal, which was the real dessert.

Small Celebrations

The happy couple, Wedding Day, 1973.

During that fall, it seemed that Kathy was indeed gathering steam and building stamina, and we all continued to relax ever so slightly. She was back at home, with visits to Dr. Lee in Boston monthly now, rather than weekly. Patrick and Liam were back at their respective schools and occupied with their seasonal sports: rugby and soccer. While she remained easily fatigued, Kathy was back at her station at the dining room table, the week's bills and sports schedules firmly in hand.

With November and Kathy and Greg's twenty-fifth wedding anniversary on the horizon, we talked about how they wanted to celebrate.

"Small and simple," is what she asked for. "I still can't plan ahead for any big do—I never know how I'm going to feel."

We settled on dinner at the Williamstown restaurant where their wedding reception had been held. There, we were happy to run into two other couples, close friends of Kathy and Greg's, seated nearby in the dining room. They made their way to our table for affectionate greetings and congratulations on the occasion.

We gathered later in the month for Thanksgiving in Arlington. We planned to have our meal together, then join Tony's family later for coffee and pie. It would be the first time his family would be seeing Kathy since her transplant. But when it came time to leave, she said she was too tired to go. She sent her regrets and stayed behind with Greg.

As it turned out, Kathy was stewarding her energies. While we were feasting on pies, she was going to bed early and getting a good sleep. The next morning, she was breakfasted and ready for the outing that she had been anticipating and preparing herself for.

For some years, the day after Thanksgiving had meant all

of us heading out together for a day of early Christmas shopping. Whether in the Berkshires or in Boston, it was a day of relaxed wandering, scouting gifts for one another with plenty of stops for snacks, with some of us pulling off in smaller groups to sit and chat while we waited for the others to catch up. The tradition was always more about the outing, spending time together, than it was about the actual shopping.

This day however, Kathy was a woman on a mission. As we roamed from store to store, she focused on the boys, her inner Santa Claus at work. By late afternoon, Greg's arms were laden with bags and Kathy had Liam trying on parkas for one of his "big" presents. The rest of us had already started to fade, with the guys more than ready to be done, and Mom parked on one of the mall benches watching the world go by until everyone was finished. I, too, had hit my saturation level with the noise and the crowds.

But Kathy wasn't finished. She left her purchases with Greg and Tony and took me by the arm for a few more stops. Too delighted to see her outlast us to complain, we shook our heads and exchanged grins of amazement. Kathy had Crate and Barrel on her radar, and we roamed the aisles for another half hour, amid the store's colorful offerings for the home. I was admiring a small pair of ivory candles with holly embedded in the wax when she snatched them from my hand.

"Great! I needed *your* Christmas present! And how about one of those glazed casserole pots? Isn't there anything else you see that you'd like?" she asked, her gaze intent.

Ah, it was the million-dollar question of course, because, as she and I both knew, all I really wanted, the only thing, was not to be found in any mall. "No, those candles would be just perfect," I said.

As she approached the register, she reached for a few tea towels in bright primary colors.

"These will be pretty in your kitchen, too. There! I think we're done!" she announced, beaming, signaling that finally, the mall-weary troops could go home.

"So, we got most of our Christmas shopping done," she announced with obvious satisfaction later at the kitchen table. "We'll just pick up a few little things for the boys' stockings and we'll be all set."

Over dinner, Greg had yet another opportunity to tease the "Little General" and we settled in for the evening, thankful for the good day, thankful to see her sorting through her bags of purchases, exhausted but pleased.

Do You Think I'm Ever Going to Get Better?

It turned out to be a good thing that she finished her Christmas shopping that day, in a burst of energy from the comet of her life force. On the morning of December 23rd, I was in our bedroom packing for our holiday trip to North Adams. We'd have time for an overnight with Kathy and Greg before the noisy but beloved extended family gathering at my cousin's on Christmas Eve. The phone rang. It was Kathy and, once again, the tone of her voice set my stomach plummeting.

"Can you come right out?" she gasped, her voice strained. "I can't talk. Trouble breathing. Greg's getting the car. Meet us at the hospital. Just come," she blurted before hanging up.

We grabbed some clothes and the bags of Christmas gifts waiting by the front door and got ourselves on the road, trying to rush, yet feeling like we were pushing through a mudslide. The drive across the state had never seemed longer. We anxiously navigated the cold, circuitous BMC garage, the familiar hospital thresholds, the maze of hallways, elevators, and waiting areas with their constant muzak and overhead pages.

When we arrived at her room, her body seemed newly shrunken, housed once more in a worn, shapeless johnnie. Kathy was felled again, slack in her hospital bed. This time, something new: she was wearing an oxygen mask.

She and Greg caught us up. They didn't know why she had suddenly become short of breath, but Dr. Spector had decided not to transfer her right away to the Brigham. After talking with Kathy and Greg, he opted to keep her local at BMC to develop a better understanding of what was going on medically and to avoid further stressing her body by the long road trip to Boston.

For days, we gathered around her bed, along with family and old friends who were in town for the holidays, and did our best to bring some cheer to her and to one another. As always, as long as I was near her, I could breathe. When we left her to go home and get some sleep, I would wake up itchy to get back to her bedside.

Tony's family again stepped in to help. Tony's brother and his wife, who lived close to the medical center, invited all of us to Christmas dinner at their house. It was totally last-minute, but they assured us there would be plenty of food, and to just come. Gratefully, after sneaking in an early morning visit, we left Kathy asleep in her room and headed to their home, beautifully decorated for the season. We felt the warmest of Christmas welcomes on a day when it was never more clear that all that mattered was love and family. After sharing their meal, we took our leave and headed right back to the hospital. At the bedside, the boys opened a few of those gifts Kathy had so carefully chosen on our recent shopping excursion.

She welcomed our company, wanted people there, then threw us out when she needed to sleep. And didn't get better.

I continued to seek out ways to stay sane. I found comfort in listening to tapes of Buddhist teacher Pema Chödrön, and tried to stay with my meditation practice, to sit and breathe through the terror of this setback. At the very least, I tried to stay present and not fly out of the room. Kathy's coping methods continued to include no-holds-barred questioning of her caretakers, along with her never-far-away humor.

There was a moment where she was on the hospital commode—we were long past any privacy being sacred—and she was hunched over in discomfort, when one eye opened to peer up at me.

"So ... where d'you think the music is coming from on the Nash Bridges barge?" she asked. I chuckled.

She was talking about the hip, funny cop show we liked, starring Don Johnson and Cheech Marin. The show's police headquarters was set on a barge in San Francisco bay, and in one of the story lines, music comes wafting into the precinct. The comic subplot involved efforts to solve the mystery of where the music was coming from. I was struck yet again with how she could still reach for something funny in these awful moments.

Somewhere in the second week of Kathy's BMC stay, I paged her oncologist, since Greg and I kept missing him during our visits. There were two problems. One was her continued low appetite, and the fact that what she did eat only seemed to cause GI problems. She would send me off to get something from one of our favorite takeout joints, only to take three bites and spend the next hour in the bathroom.

The other issue was her breathing, which was still labored and needed to be supplemented with oxygen. We were worried that there was no discernible improvement and wondered if we should be trying to get her back to her Boston team.

Dr. Spector heard me out and said, "Well, I've talked with Dr. Lee in Boston and I don't think there's anything they could or would be doing differently there right now. So, I think we're okay keeping her here, unless she really wants to go back to the Brigham."

Greg talked with her about the transfer option, and of course she preferred to remain closer to home. At BMC, it was easier for him to get to work, then be in and out with the boys, and for family and friends to visit with her. So, her Berkshire hospitalization stretched on into January.

Ten days after our conversation, Dr. Spector talked to Greg about a change of course. Now it was he who was concerned about Kathy's lack of progress and suggesting a transfer to the Brigham.

I stayed with Kathy as arrangements were made for the ambulance to transport her to Boston. It was a serious step, this shift in plans. Now there was a sense of urgency in the four-bed room they had just moved her to the night before. Room changes were just part of the chaotic life in the hospital—she had occupied so many rooms in these institutions—sometimes we left her in one place only to come back four hours later and find her someplace else. We often didn't know why the change had been made and, I sometimes thought, the hospital counted on families to be too tired to ask.

In this case the larger room had turned out to be an advantage. There was more space for the assorted staff who hustled around the bed to get her vital signs, give meds, and get transfer forms completed. At the center of all those bodies doing their discharge dance around her, Kathy was very quiet. Cooperating, but preoccupied. While challenged by the busyness happening around her, and the overhead pages and announcements, she remained focused, issuing quiet instructions and leaving little to chance.

"No don't put my slippers there—have my sister take them." And: "Those pictures of my boys can go in my blue bag. Give that to Maureen too."

The two of us were watching each other, worried, like two eyes in a storm. Then the swarm of staff moved away and we were alone.

Her expression was pensive. She peered at me, utterly still, and asked, her voice barely audible, "Maureen, do you think I'm ever going to get better?"

I rushed to reassure her.

"Of course. They'll have some ideas. They always do. Of course you will. I know you will."

Her eyes didn't leave my face, and her look—I would think about it often afterward—spoke of something she may have needed to say, that I, in my knee-jerk reaction because I could not bear the thought of her not getting better, may have cut short. The other moment I would recall later with quiet regret was her asking me in the same half whisper, her brown eyes piercing, "Do you think you could ride down in the ambulance with me?"

I missed that one too. Looking back, I see that she was afraid, perhaps afraid she wouldn't survive the trip, and wanted me there. Greg was tying up loose ends with work and the boys and would meet us at the Brigham. Instead of the yes she needed, I responded with practicality "I'd love to sweetie, but I have to take my car and drive down. If I leave it here, I won't have any way to come see you every day."

Later, with time and distance, I could see that surely there would have been a way for someone, some angel-helper to step in and drive my car to Boston so I could make the trip with her, but in the moment, it never occurred to me. In my own anxiety, I missed those signals. At such times, we are so often listening through our own shock and anxiety. Only later was I able to look back on this conversation and feel humbled to recognize another moment when my own fear clouded my ability to hear what she was *really* saying, really asking for, and to be there for her in *her* fear.

Kathy was safely transported and admitted to the Brigham and our locus once again became her room in Tower Six. I had a quiet day at home while Greg and the boys were at the hospital, visiting her. Again, I turned to pen and paper to ground myself for whatever was to come next.

Journal: January 10, 1999

Sunday. Quiet. Sitting at my desk in our newly sparkling-clean front guestroom. Tony is going to school, so I'll have some rare alone time today. Sab-

bath. To do what? To sit and stare which is what I feel like doing? To write? To make space to somehow metabolize the worry, the preoccupation, the total other-directedness of these past five or six weeks?

I curl up on the bed. The early morning light reflecting off the snow, the stately evergreens framing the bay windows, the floating white comforter all fill some soul-place inside me with peace. There is tea steeping in our little English teapot, its surface a spark of crackling yellow in the monochrome room. No morning traffic mars the stillness. Even the birds that frequent the pines seemed to be napping in the cold. I light a candle. I take in the silence, like a long-needed drink of water.

Perhaps I am resting. Perhaps I am girding myself for the next stage of the battle. With cancer, it seems that you are always girding yourself for the next battle.

There is a girlfriend-fest today, three marvelous women friends are gathering to grab a meal together and catch up. The conversation usually careens from the profound to the hilarious and back again with these women. It is always an event, and I am sorry to miss is. A part of me thinks it would be JUST the thing to do, to fill up on that rich broth of listening and laughter, yet instead, I crave only quiet.

I need to stay here and hang with this girlfriend, who needs a few hours to hear herself think, to occupy her own home and her own life, where, most *of the time now, she is just a visitor. Home for some time now has felt more like a pit stop, a place to bolt out of in the morning after downing enough oatmeal and coffee to start my engine, and to sputter back to in the evening on fumes, awake just long enough for some essentials, like showering, chatting with Tony, and checking emails, before falling back into bed again and starting all over again the next day.*

And so, a moment like this morning, in the white room's pearly light, with space for a bit of drifting, a bit of scratching with my pen, later a bit of walking in the park, has become my oxygen mask.

Tony stopped in to say good-bye before he left. He stood in the door so quietly, waiting, not wanting to startle me. When I looked up at him, I felt something rise in my chest. Again, that gratitude for having this refuge of love and home even in the midst of this heartbroken time.

February, 1999

"No Thank You"

On Friday February 5th, the now-familiar blur of Brigham interns, residents, attendings, and nurses paraded in and out of Kathy's room. The same questions and answers, repeated daily, sometimes more often, with no one moment standing out from the montage of monitoring, which was what her care had come to.

What was clear was the sinking realization once again, that even here in Boston, in the seat of some of the world's finest cancer expertise, we were still operating in trial and error mode. The most recent approach, *We don't know what's causing the breathing problems. It might be graft-versus-host, or it might be some opportunistic infection. Let's try our next best option and attack it as if it's an infection,* was still a shot in the dark. They were starting her on a combination of IV antibiotics, targeting a number of potential pathogens at once. She had been on this cocktail for several days now and there was no sign of improvement.

A young male physician appeared. He was short and earnest, with springy coils of longish hair. He sported the black-framed eyeglasses that were so ubiquitous they seemed to have been handed out on day one of medical school, along with the white coats. He positioned himself at the foot of Kathy's bed, introduced himself as a member of the surgical staff, and launched into an explanation of why he was here.

The treatment team was concerned with how things were going, he summarized, and it was obvious that so far the antibiotics were not affecting the hoped-for turnaround. The only other recourse, he explained, was surgical.

"What we'd like to do next is to take you to the OR to get a lung biopsy." His voice was enthusiastic, persuasive, as if he was convinced about the course he had come to offer.

"It's the only way for us to be sure of what it is we're treating. We had hoped to avoid it, and of course with your breathing already compromised, anesthesia will need to do their own assessment to determine whether or not they feel comfortable, but we'd like to do it as soon as—"

"No, thank you."

Before he could finish his thought about whether indeed the anesthesia department would even risk taking Kathy to the OR, Kathy's voice, barely audible, yet conveying all the authority of a lifetime, stopped him.

The young surgeon paused in mid-pitch, his face dropping its pro-forma professional mask momentarily and registering a mix of genuine confusion and concern. His hands, which had been gesticulating for emphasis as he made his case, ducked into the pockets of his white coat.

Quickly retrieving his doctorly demeanor, he launched another volley of explanations, this time accentuating the gravity of the situation in case Kathy was not aware. His voice was urgent as he pointed out that the window to pursue a biopsy was closing by the minute. They were hoping to book the OR for that afternoon.

This time, Kathy listened gravely until he finished. On

the beat of his closing syllable, she repeated herself, ever so slightly increasing her volume, and adding a touch of formality as if it might help to get through to him.

"I'd like to decline, thank you."

The room was absolutely still as the two faced off. The serious, bespectacled young doctor, with his name and institutional logos emblazoned across his white coat like rows of military ribbons. With a roped-up stethoscope dangling from one pocket, a wad of notes, presumably about the patients he was visiting, leaking from the other, he exuded the borrowed confidence of his appointment to this famed institution. And he looked to be maybe six years older than Patrick, Kathy's eldest.

Kathy, hair shorn and face gaunt from the journey, held her head high, her will naked and clear now. Her eyes were kind, yet determined, as she met his gaze without flinching.

"No thank you," she spoke once again into the stunned silence. So polite even as she brushed him away.

"But ..." He appeared to falter, his face paling.

"I know. I understand," she softened her voice slightly for the young man, as if allowing him to catch up with her. The whole encounter leading to this moment, which felt as if the world turning on its axis had let out a terrible groan as it came grinding to a halt, took place in a matter of minutes. Maybe three. Maybe five.

The air in the small room was charged with something beyond silence. A moment of eternity was unfolding, as they do all day, every day in the frenetic midst of a big city hospital. But this particular moment was defined by my sister and her extraordinary will, her soft, clear voice saying those three words: *No thank you.*

Minutes after the young surgeon left, Dr. Lee appeared in Kathy's room—no coincidence, I'm sure. Like Kathy, I always felt relieved to see her. Her simple presence calmed something in me. Only in hindsight would I recognize that this time, my relief was also tinged with hope, hope that she would somehow be able to talk Kathy out of the decision she had just quietly announced.

But she was not. In fact, she didn't even try. She began a delicate foray into the question of the surgical biopsy, and instantly Kathy shook her head. "I'm just so tired. I can't do any more."

Then Kathy turned to face me. I was standing by her bedside, stunned speechless with the implications of what I was hearing. Looking up at me now, her face was blotchy with emotion, her eyes grave, plaintive, utterly unguarded. No twinkle. No wry quip. Just her utter focus, asking the most solemn question of her life.

"Is it okay, do you think? If I stop? Will you be mad at me? Will everyone be mad at me?" she asked.

The answer came from my depths in response to hers. I reached two hands out. One to her shoulder, the other found her hand. The answer came without any thought, instantly arriving out of the center of my chest, fully formed.

"Of course not, sweetie. Of course not. There is not one of us who could do what you have *already* done. You get to decide. You've fought so hard. You do what you need to, and we're all going to be right here with you."

Kathy nodded.

"I'm just so tired," she repeated in a voice so weak as to leave no doubt. She asked me to call Greg. And Kevin. "I think Kevin should come now," she whispered. Then she closed her eyes, retreating inside.

In moments, Dr. Lee and I were out in the middle of the hall, near the nursing station. She said nothing but turned to me and opened her arms. The top of her head just about reached my chin, yet I tumbled toward her and the emotion that had been frozen in my throat broke through as I reached her. I knew that Kathy's breathing was getting worse. I knew that, outside of the surgical biopsy, we were out of treatment options.

"Does this mean it will be soon?" I choked out the unthinkable question. She held my gaze and nodded, then answered gently. "A few days maybe."

Here was the moment there is no preparing for. The moment I—or any of us who had been walking this journey alongside Kathy—had held firmly at bay. No matter how bad things had seemed, it had been nearly impossible to contemplate that we could come to this. It seems so obvious, of course, looking back. But then, if I thought about the boys for even a second, or about Greg, or my Mom, facing the loss of her daughter? I had been unable to stay with any of these possibilities for longer than seconds.

And for myself, having felt her presence literally or figuratively beside me for 46 of my 47 years, when I finally let in the prospect of that loss, I went to pieces. Once again, Dr. Lee made this moment part of her work. She did not brush it aside or cut it short with murmurs of other things she had to do. Her own eyes glistening, she stayed present with me in that awful moment of realization. I was deeply grateful for her—what can only be called love—love for her patients and their families, attending to bodies and spirits with utter professionalism and compassion. She stood in the middle of that nursing station and she held me, first in an embrace, then by the hands, making space in the midst of the high-tech medical care, for grief.

Then, once more, coming back to what Kathy needed, we made a plan to gather the people Kathy loved, and to honor her wishes. I went to phone Greg, back in North Adams, so he could pack up my mom and the boys. I phoned Tony. I phoned Kevin. *Come, everyone. It's time to come.* I phoned my work to restart my remaining family leave. Then I drifted to the chapel and sat and stared as if girding for what lay ahead. Beyond any more tears by then, I made my way back to Kathy's room where she slept. It was a simple comfort to re-join her at the bedside, to take her hand, and just be with her.

We had begun what would later seem to me, Holy Week.

Seeing the Crab

Kathy dozed off and on, then later that afternoon, she wanted to talk. Again, she brought up the memoir by Christina Middlebrook called "Seeing the Crab," the story of Middlebrook's own harrowing, albeit successful journey through breast cancer, including an autologous or self-donor bone marrow transplant.

Kathy's current hospital room was adjacent to the transplant area, a semi-private room that thankfully she had to herself. In contrast with the windowless enclosure of the nearby pod where she had spent two months, this room was large, airy even. Brightened with pastel plaid curtains, it offered a generous helping of natural light from the wall of windows facing out over the busy Longwood Avenue hospital corridor. Keeping the door closed had become a reflex, to give us more quiet. Just beyond the door, the standing army of staffers navigated a hallway clogged with laundry and medical carts, wheelchairs and gurneys, while patients and family members gingerly walked the corridors as their only means of exercise. The hospital scents had already become background to us. Everything smelled of sanitizer and a too-close space full of bodies. And heat. The building was kept so warm that the rooms smelled, too, of heat.

I sat perched on Kathy's hospital bed, which she had moved up into the sitting position. She told me about a moment in Middlebrook's book where one of the author's friends, herself gravely ill, tells her, "My only regret, the only thing I wish, is that I hadn't spent so much time feeling guilty."

Kathy paused, her eyes somber, her thin neck lost in the limp, oversized johnnie. Her lips, coated with salve to keep them from cracking, pursed before she spoke again, as if she was unsure whether to say what she was about to say.

"That's how *I* feel," she told me, watching my face closely. For, as she seemed to suspect, I was startled by this. She had never talked with me before about feeling guilty.

"Honey, what on earth would you ever have to feel guilty *about*?!" I asked, my heart sinking.

"Oh," Kathy shrugged, "You know ... we women feel guilty about all these little things."

About what? About what? My mind now shakes a fist at me, wondering again why I didn't press her further. But I didn't. My instinct once more was protective. Protective of her? Or of me? Instead of further questioning, which might have given her a chance to reveal some corner of the trouble in her heart, once again I offered a quick reassurance.

I put my hand over hers and said, my voice wavering, "Kathy, you haven't one thing on this earth to feel guilty about. You are the most amazing friend and wife, and mother to those boys. You have done everything you could possibly do to give them a life filled with love."

She nodded. "I do feel good about that," she whispered back. "Of course, I have such great boys."

"And they *got* to be great boys because of Greg and you." Now my eyes were locked onto hers, my tone fierce with wanting to be sure she could see this. Kathy nodded back. The dark fringe of her grown-in curls was matted and askew, her face pink with emotion, soft and open. Her eyes were glistening, and they searched mine as if desperate to get some final things clear. Huddled almost nose-to-nose, we were suddenly in the heart of loss.

"And a sister," I told her. "*What a sister.* I hope to God you haven't wasted one second feeling guilty about that one either, because no one, *no one*, could ever have been a better sister to me than you have. I am the luckiest sister on the planet."

"Thanks," she answered, holding my gaze for a beat more. Then she whispered, "Maybe if there's reincarnation, we'll get to do this again sometime. Only this time I won't get sick and die young, and we'll get to be old ladies knitting together in the nursing home like we're supposed to."

Streaming tears, I nodded and held her arm. Wisecrack or wish, her words settled over us like a prayer we were saying together.

Then, sensing that Kathy was not finished working out these last details, I asked, "Is there anything else I can do, or that you want to talk about?"

"Yeah, just don't have my funeral breakfast at St. Joseph's Court—please!"

A flicker of a gleam returned to her eyes, since a reference to this moment in our family history usually guaranteed a smile. When Mom and I had returned home from Dad's funeral, we had regaled her with the story, which soon became part of the family lore, concerning The Funeral Breakfast at St. Joseph's Court That Took So Long We Expected Someone Else to Expire During It.

At St. Joseph's Court, the senior housing my Mom lived in, the dining room was operated by a Berkshire developmental disabilities program with the kind of TLC that a five-star restaurant couldn't buy. Mom would walk into the windowless basement-level dining room, brightened with cheery wallpaper and silk flowers, and be greeted by her favorite server Diane calling out, "Hey Millie! I've got your tea water ready for you, nice and hot just like you like it!"

But on the occasion of my Dad's funeral breakfast, the usually good-humored staff was over-taxed and the kitchen was overwhelmed. The result was, to put it mildly, a breakfast that seemed to arrive by slow train. I remember looking down the long table, lined with pale-faced mourners who had been up since early morning for the 8 a.m. funeral mass. The good-natured small talk had petered out and the guests were eyeing the doorway longingly, hoping to spot a plate of hot eggs or simply a pile of toast on the horizon. When two earnest servers finally appeared, my uncles broke into applause. The applause proved to be somewhat premature however, since the eggs turned out to be cold.

When we first told Kathy the story, my mother and I, exhausted and punchy after all the funeral gatherings and travel, had laughed so hard that we'd cried. Today, as Kathy made her own small joke about it, we wondered what our ever-hungry father would have had to say about his funeral breakfast.

"Yeah, can't you just hear Daddy?" I asked her. "He'd have been telling them, 'Don't worry yourselves with hurrying now. If you wait just a little bit longer, they won't be needing their eggs anymore and you can just call Flynn the undertaker to come and collect them, and they can join me at the cemetery!'"

Suddenly, Kathy became serious again.

"I do have one thing," she said, her breathing starting to strain. "You can really talk to people, and you have a way of making them feel better. Would you do my eulogy?"

Two flashes, contradictory. First, the instinct to do anything and everything to reassure her and to minimize her suffering in any way I could. Right behind it, the feeling that I could have buried my head in her blankets and howled or bolted from the room at her request.

I squeaked out something like: *Of course.* And: *My honor.*

Then the enormity of what we were discussing seemed to overtake her again. She glanced up and noticed the pictures of the boys pinned to the wall in front of her bed. (Soon, the nurses would suggest removing them. When people are in their last days, it can alleviate some distress, they told us, to remove reminders of those they are leaving behind.) She closed her eyes again and asked for her medication.

I felt a surge of panic, realizing that once the Ativan kicked in, she would sleep. Our conversation would be over, and at this point, every conversation bore the weight of possibly being the last. I stifled an urge to shake her and say, "Don't go to sleep! Stay here with me!" Instead I sat back in the chair, bereft.

Kathy was not finished, however. She opened her eyes and arched an eyebrow at me, "You remember too, you're gonna help Greg? With the boys? Promise?"

"You know it, Kath. I'll be all over them. Wild horses will not keep me away," I promised, grateful for this charge, which I would have taken up anyway.

"And one more thing?" her voice was weakening now, "Remember that lady? That lady you told me about? When he's ready, will you take Greg to see her?" I was baffled for a moment. What lady? *Was she talking with me about fixing Greg up?*

"The smoking lady," she said, seeing my confusion. "Take him to the smoking lady, will you?" She had tucked away the memory of an unconventional healer Tony had seen years ago. In two visits, she had helped him—as she had many others—to stop smoking.

After taking care of all these matters that were on her mind, Kathy fell asleep and I sat watching her for a bit before heading off to call Tony. After the events of the afternoon, I badly needed to see the other person I turned to when things were almost more than I could bear.

I waited for him in the hallway outside the Brigham cafeteria. As usual, I had no trouble spotting him. His tall frame made him easy to pick out in a crowd, even in the blur of people going in and out at dinnertime. I ran to him and buried my face in his shoulder for a few moments, both of us oblivious to the foot traffic around us. Then we took the familiar Tower elevators to Kathy's sixth-floor room, where she greeted him, searching his face as she had mine, for acceptance.

"I'm so tired. I don't have an ounce left in me to fight anymore," she announced by way of hello. Tony leaned over and enfolded her in his long arms, gently reassuring her that he understood.

Dr. Lee appeared again. Earlier in the day she had broken the news to us that she would be leaving tomorrow for a week, flying out to a transplant conference on the west coast. To state the obvious, this was very hard to hear.

She told Kathy, "Next week will be an important week, and I'm sorry I won't be here with you." She said that a colleague, who we didn't know at all, would be covering for her and that she would leave him with explicit instructions as to Kathy's wishes. She asked again about the ventilator—had Kathy changed her mind, if her breathing got worse? Kathy remained firm. No vent. Dr. Lee said she would leave orders to continue with full antibiotics in a last-ditch hope that the lung issues might yet respond.

When Kathy asked, Dr. Lee told us that things looked a bit worse on her most recent chest x-rays. I asked if we would be getting any more information about what was causing Kathy's breathing problems.

"Not likely," she told me. "We probably have all the information we're going to have." She promised they would keep Kathy comfortable and continue to supplement her breathing with more oxygen as she needed it.

Just then, Greg and the boys and my mom arrived. Dr. Lee spent more time with us, meeting first with the adults, then including Patrick and Liam, to review what she had discussed with Kathy and address any questions. Her manner was brief, simple, and compassionate.

When we rejoined Kathy, she seemed visibly relieved. She loved Dr. Lee and I could sense her relief that she had been able to talk to her sons, finding words that in this moment were no doubt too painful for her to find herself. Kathy looked into the boys' faces and asked, "Do you have any other questions?" They shook their heads quietly before taking up their seats by her side.

Each of these moments felt, as they were happening, holy. Holy moments. Each of us wanted more than anything to give her peace in any way we could. While she wanted desperately to be sure that we would all be okay, that we understood, and that we would be able to survive, even if we ourselves had, as yet, no idea how.

The next day, Sunday, I stayed at home as a small posse of Kathy's hometown family and best friends drove in from North Adams. When I arrived later, I found Kathy's nurse keeping an eye on things, and Kathy sitting up in bed, oxygen tube in place, visiting with a few of her near and dear. With a small crowd gathered in the family room, we had to dole out what precious time was left with her. I fluttered in the background, wanting to make sure that Mom and Greg and the boys got into the room as much as possible. As her old friends visited, she quizzed them about their own kids and how their lives were going. There was no talk of what was happening to hers.

To those who hadn't been there all along, she must have looked very weak, but we saw her rally and rise in a way that was unmistakable. She wanted one last visit with her people, and by God, she was going to have it.

There were no big tearful goodbyes. Her leave-taking with them was almost casual. One of her oldest friends paused at the door and Kathy told her, "Okay take care then, I'll be in touch."

Later on, when this friend's eldest son got a job he really wanted in Denver, she would tell me she felt sure that Kathy had somehow helped, that she was keeping "in touch."

At the end of the afternoon, a few of Kathy's friends and I sat together in the small lobby near the Tower Six elevators. Her friend Debbie was a longtime ICU staffer at the hospital in North Adams, and she lingered behind to have a conversation with the night nurse. Debbie reported that they were considering giving Kathy a BiPap (Bilevel Positive Airway Pressure) mask, a device typically used to treat sleep apnea. The mask covers the nose and mouth and facilitates breathing by increasing air pressure into the throat and lungs.

Kathy's increased discomfort with breathing had not been apparent to us, but it showed up in her blood oxygen levels. I was momentarily relieved that they had a solution. But Debbie also explained the downside; the device blows the air in "as if you were riding in the car with your face out the window," she told us. "And it straps on tightly over the nose and mouth, so you can't talk," she added. A mix of grief that Kathy was obviously failing further, and panic—*no more talking?!*—shot through me.

We were in a new land now, where every setback was permanent. The three of us, friends since we were girls, held one another on the hallway bench near the windows as darkness fell over the city below us.

Touched by an Angel

After all the friends left, things got very quiet and, pretty quickly, very intense. Toward dinnertime, it became clear that while Kathy was getting the maximum oxygen possible through the tube, she was increasingly short of breath.

Since it was a Sunday evening, only a handful of staff were around to call the shots. The team decided to go forward with the BiPap mask. With Kathy's nurse, the young attending doctor, and the respiratory technician circling her, the changeover from the oxygen tube to the mask began. The room was tense as they monitored Kathy's oxygen numbers, which were dangerously low. To add to the worry, she had begun to have some heart symptoms, with her heart rate climbing during the process.

Once the mask was on, however, she lay back against her pillows, resting, and for the moment stabilized, better than they had hoped.

The young attending, tall and lanky, asked if he could speak with Greg and me to discuss "how we see things developing, and prognosis." His face was tight and the papers in his hand shook ever so slightly. It crossed my mind to wonder how much experience he could have had with this kind of Sunday afternoon family meeting.

He took us into the conference room next to the unit and told us that while Kathy was "tolerating the mask exceptionally well," there was concern about her overall lung function, and her heart was working extremely hard to keep up.

"The bottom line is that she could die tonight," he told us.

The room began to spin. However much we had begun preparing ourselves, watching Kathy hold court at her bedside that afternoon had not left us anticipating that we had so little time left.

A number of reactions bombarded me. *Her heart??* Her heart. There had been all manner of issues with her respiratory, GI, and neurological systems. We hadn't thought to worry about her heart. The doctor then met briefly with my mom and the boys to share this same information. There was nothing anyone could do or say to soften the blow. *How would they ever get over this moment?* I wondered. And then, oddly, I became concerned about the doctor. He seemed so nervous himself. *So young,* I thought. *So young, to have this responsibility.* In spite of the terrible message he came bearing, I had to resist the urge to reach out and touch his arm, to comfort him.

As I returned to her bedside in the quiet room, Kathy opened her eyes, her face grave. "Is it okay? Can I go home now?" she asked, her voice scarcely a whisper.

Taking her question literally I demurred, "Oh sweetie, that might be too much for you now. You're all set up here, and the nurses here know just how to take care of you to keep you comfortable. And we're all right here with you. One of us will keep staying with you all the time. Will that be Ok?"

She closed her eyes.

"I want to go home now," she repeated. As she spoke, her nurse stepped into the room. She caught my eye and whispered. "She may not be talking about her physical home. Patients often begin talking about 'going home' as they near the end of their time."

I had completely missed that meaning but instantly wanted to correct my response. I leaned close. "Sorry if I didn't understand just now. And it's okay for you to go home, Kath. It's okay darlin'," I said, using the endearment our mom often called us. And in that moment, I meant it. It had been a long journey and now the end was near. Kathy was signaling that she was ready, and we continued to struggle to keep up with her.

The family regathered to find that after the high emotion of the last hour, a palpable sense of peace had fallen over the room. Some new softening was present, with everyone empty, for the moment, of tears. As dusk fell, the sole light came from a table lamp which lent the space a peach-colored glow. We pulled chairs near to Kathy's bed and closed the door once more against the beeping and clanging in the hallway outside.

It turned out that, given her outsized will, Kathy was still able to talk with the mask on. Though her speech was slightly muffled, we could clearly understand her, which was an enormous relief. She lay with her eyes closed, breathing more peacefully now, yet alert enough that she would pipe up periodically to join the muted bedside conversation.

At one point while her nurse was tending to her, she announced, "I want to be sure to watch *Touched by an Angel*. It's on at eight!"

Kathy was a fan of the popular TV show, featuring Irishwoman Roma Downey and Della Reese as angels. Each week the duo and their male sidekick would find someone who, knowingly or not, was living in the vicinity of impending death. Sometimes the person lived; often they died, but always with some important unfinished business attended to, thanks to their angelic helpers. I wondered to myself whether the storyline had been providing Kathy some kind of solace over the past few months.

Once the show came on, however, Kathy hardly seemed to watch it. Perhaps the background soundtrack of the familiar plot line provided some comfort. Her boys were nearby, hopping up to soak a warm facecloth to wash her face, or to mix mouthwash with cold water to swab her mouth. Both awkward and tender with their tasks, they wanted to help her any way they could. It reminded me of my childhood experiences of helping out in sick rooms, and while at the time I was probably wide-eyed and a bit overwhelmed, I felt a new appreciation for having been brought into the room as a youngster, even when death was nearby.

The feeling at the bedside was amazingly settled-down, cozy even. The news we had gotten only hours ago had broken each of our hearts, yet seeing her in such a peaceful state was deeply comforting. A sense of togetherness took over, with all of us gathered, nurses in and out frequently, and the TV show about the angels on in the background. The room was filled with tenderness, all directed toward Kathy.

She continued to doze off and on. She woke to ask what time Kevin was flying in from the northwest. Greg and I exchanged glances, each wondering, we shared later, if she was waiting for him. At another point, her eyes had been closed for forty minutes or so and we were speaking in whispers when Tony mentioned the young woman who had won Gold at last winter's Olympics. We had watched her skate a year ago as we'd waited with Kathy in the Family Room for her admission to the Transplant Unit.

"What was her name?" Tony wondered, speaking softly so as not to disturb her.

From behind her mask, not even bothering to open her eyes, Kathy called out, "Tara Lipinski!" Everyone laughed. Though we thought she had "checked out" for a while, she was still right there, taking in what was going on, and as always, right on top of her sports info.

Toward bedtime, as we readied to go, I felt a rising wave of panic at the idea of leaving her. I realized I couldn't. Everyone else was talking quietly, finding coats, saying good night to Greg and Patrick, who were staying overnight with her. That was when I came face-to-face with the very real fear that once we left, Kathy may not be there when we returned.

Fortunately, Tony was watching and noticed the frantic expression on my face. Taking my arm, he stepped me out into the nursing station.

"I can't leave ... I can't!" I heard the words coming out of my mouth before I even realized where I was going with them. "I have to be closer. We all have to be. What if ..." The rest of the thought disappeared into Tony's shoulder. We quickly began weighing the possibility of staying overnight at the nearby Best Western.

This was not an easy plan for several reasons, including the fact that Mom didn't have her heart medications with her. But we quickly figured it out between us and arrived at a decision, thanks to Tony's patience and kindness. He didn't hesitate for a moment to offer to check us into the hotel, then drive back to our house in Arlington to fetch Mom's meds and anything else we needed, so everyone could stay the night right around the corner.

One More Chat

The following afternoon Kathy alternated between physical restlessness and stretches of dozing. They had started to give her Fentanyl to ease her discomfort, so her conscious moments were becoming more sporadic. Her breathing eased and she appeared more peaceful, so we took turns slipping away to grab some sleep.

Kevin arrived, coming straight from Logan airport. He took a seat next to Kathy, and was thankfully able to talk with her a bit, BiPap mask and all. She continued to doze on and off.

At one point, she woke and asked for Greg. I told her he was off sleeping. He'd been there all night at her bedside, folded up into the uncomfortable hospital chair.

"Do you want me to call him?" I asked.

"Yeah. Please. I like having everyone here." she answered.

Of course. She was already operating on a different clock than the rest of us. An eternity clock. How important could sleep be from her point of view?

So, groggy as she was, there remained moments of lucidity and, even still, of humor.

Kathy's transplant nurse Toni stopped by again late in the afternoon on her way off duty. The room was a refuge now, a chamber of peace. Kathy was dozing.

Toni leaned in, putting her face close to Kathy's and crooned, "Hi there, sweetie."

Her voice was tender, her flame-hued hair riotous beside Kathy's face, which was as pale and translucent as the mother-of-pearl seashells she loved to collect as a little girl.

Hearing Toni's voice, Kathy's eyes blinked open.

Toni had recently visited western Massachusetts and she chatted with Kathy about being out on her home turf. Then she began to draw out a story about our wedding day, something Kathy had obviously shared in one of their conversations during the long days on the transplant unit.

"So, you and Tony had your wedding out in western Massachusetts, right?" she asked, one hand clasping Kathy's shoulder, while she turned to me, eyes smiling encouragement.

Kathy looked at me, gesturing with a nod and a slow smile. Her eyes said, *you tell her.*

"And what was the name of that place? It had a funny name if I remember ..." Toni continued.

I said the funny name of the place: "Stump Sprouts."

Toni grinned, nudging Kathy softly as if they were fellow conspirators.

"And, I heard that Maureen was *late* for her own wedding?" Toni asked, ribbing me, her eyes fixed on Kathy's in joint mischief-making.

Kathy's slight smile widened at the chance to play along. She gave a big, solid nod and whispered, "Yeah, right!"

Now Toni winked in my direction, milking it. "So ... wasn't it, like 100 degrees in the shade or something?" she continued, building her story.

"Right!" Kathy nodded. "And humid! Real humid!" she whispered.

"And, didn't ya think, that she could've begun getting ready a little sooner?" Toni teased, her voice animated.

Kathy nodded enthusiastically. "I *know!*" Her head and shoulders rose in a soft approximation of a chuckle, and Toni and I joined her.

Then Kathy's voice again, tender, "She's getting better, though."

It was our last conversation together. One last sister chat, in which this skilled nurse—no wonder we call them angels—had given us both a gift. She had stopped by at the end of a grueling day spent ushering yet another patient through a transplant to see Kathy one final time. I had offered to step out for a bit so she could have time alone with her, but Toni said, "No, stay." And as she helped Kathy tease me one last time, picking up our lifelong banter and having a small chuckle in the shadow of the terrible separation to come, she showed a level of caring and generosity that flies far above any job description.

Even when you "know" that someone is dying, it is nearly impossible to comprehend that any given conversation may be the last. You keep thinking, or at least I did, that the person will awaken one more time and there will be one more chance for words. Then, at some point, they don't. And there aren't. And those final conversations become sacred text, seared into memory. That evening was the last time Kathy was able to speak with us. God bless Toni, for the thousandth time, for helping us to have that final sisters' visit.

Surrender

Over the next day the BiPap mask became a focus, because it wasn't fitting correctly and the longer she wore it, the more this became an issue. It was slipping around on her face, and she developed a tiny cut on the bridge of her nose from the friction. I insisted that they find a smaller size, causing tension with the harried respiratory therapist, who was in and out of the room, while the nurse manager loomed outside the door, watching it all with a worried look on her face. Although we weren't aware of it at the time, the decision to use the BiPap at that time was somewhat controversial, because it could extend her life. Whatever discussions were taking place in the privacy of the nursing station, we just wanted to see her more comfortable.

The new mask the respiratory therapist brought was child-sized, and it crushed Kathy's nose right where she already had a cut. I got into a tussle with the therapist, insisting there had to be a size that would work better. She likewise insisted there was virtually no difference between the two masks we had already tried. The tone of her voice inferred that I was being a difficult, demanding family member. She held the masks side by side, one on Kathy's face, one in her hands.

"See? They're the same," she snapped. "Do you still want me to change it again (*You pain in the ass*)?!"

"Yes," I insisted.

It was obvious to me that the new mask was too small. I tried to soften my approach by smiling at the therapist. I knew how hard people worked in these places, and as snitty as we'd just gotten with each other, I wanted try to show my appreciation.

My strategy didn't help. I had the feeling that this sort of end-of-life situation was not something she had to deal with regularly and was outside her comfort zone. This spillover of tension from the hospital staff had, amazingly, never happened during our lengthy dealings with the Brigham. Finally, after all our back and forth, she left to look for another size. She returned, with yet a third mask. It was instantly, obviously, better.

She left the child-sized mask behind on the bed-stand and I looked at it after she departed, still in a huff. There was a small 'P' in the front of the child-sized mask, and a small 'S' on the new one. I checked the nostril opening on the discarded mask. It was much tinier, as was the opening where it fit over the nose, despite the roughly same-sized exterior. The new mask no longer slipped, and Kathy stopped pulling at it in her sleep. She quieted, and I was glad I made the fuss.

In case we weren't already operating on our last nerves, Kathy's two nurses came to us later that afternoon, concerned. Like so many of our conversations, this one took place in the glassed-in ante-space outside of her room, with Greg, Mom, and me lined up in the steamy quarters, speaking in hushed tones to the two nurses. As usual, their approach was full of straight talk laced with love, and in this instance, concern that their patient's wishes were getting lost in the shuffle.

"Her respirations are increasingly rapid and shallow, and her heart is working hard to keep up. She's borderline ventable now," one of them told us. "The resident just wrote orders for a "full code." If her condition worsened, the order mandated the loudspeaker announcement of a "code," summoning staff with a crash cart to make the most aggressive possible interventions to forestall death. It also meant placing the patient on a ventilator, which Kathy had made quite clear she never wanted again.

We felt blindsided by this news. All of us knew what Kathy's wishes were, and they did not include the full-out heroics of a code. They also raised concerns about her continued treatment with IV antibiotics.

"It's a little different in nursing than it is in medicine," one of the nurses explained. "In medicine, it's more aggressive. I asked the attending this morning, 'Do we need to keep pouring all these antibiotics into her? We can see they're not doing any good in terms of her respiratory issues and they're simply taxing her organs more to process and excrete them.' And he said, "That's what the family wants. They want this treated as aggressively as possible, so that's what we'll do.'"

I was suddenly missing Dr. Lee's clear, steady presence sharply.

We were both alarmed and dismayed. We had felt assured when she left that Dr. Lee had thoroughly reviewed Kathy's wishes and left clear orders in the chart. Why was this conversation even happening? As we would later learn, there are many nuances to such end-of-life conversations which make it challenging to anticipate every possibility, timeline, and option. And sometimes, as in this case, even with the finest of care and intentions, clarity can get lost in the relaying of information.

In any case, we were left with the question of what to do.

To call a stop to the antibiotics meant no longer waiting and "giving it a little more time," but taking decisive action. Action that signaled surrender. Final surrender. We went back and forth, agonized. On one hand, maybe with just one more day, just a little more time, the drugs might turn the tide and save her.

Yet hadn't her fully lucid decision only a few days ago to refuse a lung biopsy indicated exactly where she stood on the question of further aggressive treatment?

It had been five days on the IVs. There should have been some evidence of response or improvement by now, and there was none. Which meant that whatever was going on with Kathy's lungs, it was not an infection. Our last shot had been diagnosis by massive infusion of antibiotics. And we were confronting the heart-rending reality: the trial had failed. While it had been one thing to make peace with Kathy's decision not to pursue the lung biopsy, it was another to take the step of halting the antibiotics.

There was nothing more medicine had to offer, except narcotics to keep her "comfortable." As much as things had been spiraling downward these last days, the anesthesia of denial had a stubborn hold. Confronted with the final reality, we struggled at every step, feeling blindsided anew each time we had to make a decision.

Ultimately it was my mother, the former nurse, who

stepped forward to speak the truth that was settling over our hearts but which neither Greg nor I could yet say. She assumed her role as matriarch. A matriarch in puffy sneakers and lavender polyester whose lifetime of devotion and struggle gave her the spiritual strength in that moment to lead her family. Standing only three-quarters of the height of the rest of the adults in the circle, she reached for my arm and for Greg's. Her voice shook as she confronted the matter head-on.

"Kathy is dying. And there isn't a thing more we can do about it! We have to help her let go now."

It was a terrible moment. Something collapsed in our little circle. Maybe it was hope. Maybe it was denial. As we held one another, a shift took place and we began to come to grips, to catch up with Kathy, who had told us days ago that she was ready.

Together, we made the decision to stop trying to treat her. Her medical care would now be solely focused on her comfort. Shortly after the discussion, Kathy's nurse returned and, scarcely making a sound, removed all but one of the many IV bags around the bed.

After the last two years in which every ounce of energy that every person in that room could summon had been directed at helping Kathy win back her life, a sense of finality fell over us. The fight was over. Now our task was to accompany her into this next and final terrain, to walk with her to the end.

Sleepover

It was my turn to stay over with Kathy, but when it came time for me to hunker into one of the visitor chairs for the night, Kathy's night nurse was having none of it. She knew where the stash of plastic cots was kept, and toward bedtime she took my arm like a bossy auntie and dragged me through the back rooms and dark storage spaces on the sixth floor, insisting I lie down on each of the various options to test them out.

"You might as well be comfortable," she shrugged. "Try this one. Which one feels the best?"

At around eleven o'clock, I threw myself down on the cot I'd chosen, grateful to the nurse for the time and effort she'd taken. I also felt a kind of contentment in having this time alone with my sister, which felt intimate, even though by this point she was receiving so much morphine that she was unresponsive. Content is a funny word to use, but it captures the sense that this was clearly, exactly, utterly, where I wanted to be. Liam and my mom were too young and too old, respectively, to stay, and Greg and Patrick had spent the last two nights curled up in visitor's chairs and were desperate for a real night's sleep, so it worked for everyone. As exhausted as we all were, there was a sense of accord among us, that each was doing what he or she needed to with a sense of purposefulness and love. I had no belongings with me since I hadn't planned to stay. Still, I had a sense of having everything I needed: a toothbrush, a bathroom, a facecloth, a cot, a blanket, and my sister.

As she dozed quietly, I leaned over and whispered to her. We had all continued talking to her even after she could no longer respond.

"I'm staying right next to you tonight, sweetie. We'll have a sleepover just like we did when we were little."

I kissed her forehead, which was warm and clammy, then closed all the blinds, lay down on the cot, and crashed.

Falling asleep beside Kathy was oddly sweet and peaceful and I slept deeply for a while. But in the middle of the night I woke suddenly, and sat up, alert. I moved to the bedside and sat with her for a long while, reaching under the blanket to hold her hand and whisper to her. Some long litany came to me, more reassurances to her about Patrick and Liam, telling her how bravely she had fought, that we all understood, and that we would be okay. I read a bit to her from a Stephen Levine book I'd kept in my bag, then found some words of my own.

"We'll take care of each other. You just lean into God now, Sweetie. Just lean into God and know that you are held and safe there, and whenever it's time for you to let go, just go, into the light. Just relax into it and let yourself go ..."

Near dawn I fell back to sleep, my chair pulled up close to the bed and my pillow beside her face. I awoke when the nurse came to check on her.

"It won't be long now. Sometime this morning probably," she told me. "We can tell because her kidneys are slowing down."

And then: "We were talking out back tonight, the staff, and saying we all wished when it's our time that we have a family like yours. And a sister like you. You're a *good sister*."

I shook my head sleepily.

"No, I got to be Kathy's sister, you have no idea. *I'm* the lucky one," I answered as the nurse folded me into her large self for a goodbye hug.

These last few days had sometimes felt harsh with fatigue, sometimes shocking with the changes taking place in Kathy. But a softening had taken place over the last day. At dawn, high above the city, the night sky first turned mauve, then apricot, and then became a blazing blue. Inside, the space felt as if it had been swept with incense and lit with candles.

A new nurse came on shift. She spoke to Kathy, her voice gentle, her every gesture communicating tenderness. "Kathy? When I come back, we're going to clean you up and make you a little more comfortable, okay?"

She asked me if I wanted to take a shower. But after brushing my teeth and washing my face, I felt refreshed. While the nurses were there, I slipped out for a few minutes to head downstairs for coffee. The hospital was starting to wake, the muted sounds of the night replaced by the hum of day staff and patients pouring through the massive revolving front doors.

Kathy's blood pressure and body temperature had been dropping. I knew from what the night nurse had said that it would be soon, yet as we sailed into a new day, the sun pouring light outside in the street, I also had some doubt. It seemed so unlikely she would go in the bright daylight and I wondered whether it would perhaps be tonight or tomorrow.

Back in her room, I remembered the new nightgown I had tucked away in my bag after buying it for her a few weeks ago. I dug it out and unfolded the thick blue flannel plaid with small red buttons down the front. So the little efforts did count. It mattered after all that I had grabbed fifteen extra minutes on one of those crazy days to dash into a shop and buy her a real nightgown. And that I kept schlepping it around with me in my hospital satchel, sensing that at some point she might want it. Because here was the moment.

The two nurses, busy straightening the fresh sheets and brushing her hair, saw it and smiled. "Oh sure, of course, let's put that on her!" As they changed her, they lifted and turned her deftly, so light was she, as if she were a small bird. The task complete, we all sighed. She looked so much softer and more Kathy, with her hair fluffed up and the red buttons catching the sunlight.

I told her, "We've got your brand-new blue flannel nightie on you. You look so pretty!"

Knowing the end was close, I asked the nurse, "Will you keep this on her? She wouldn't want to be back in one of those johnnies." At the end, these small things seemed important. Things I knew Kathy would want.

And she assured me, "Of course we will."

Greg and Patrick arrived. Tony planned to follow with Mom and Liam. While Patrick and the nurses stayed with Kathy, Greg and I went downstairs to the coffee shop, and we talked about the arrangements we needed to plan, for after she passed. It was a calm, sad, loving conversation. A conversation that only a month before would have reduced us to hysterics, we now had tiredly, clearly, simply, because it was the next thing we needed to do for her.

Shortly after we returned to Kathy's room, Greg left again with Patrick, to have breakfast in the cafeteria. We had a sense of being alert to her changes, but not of urgency.

They were only gone for ten minutes when Kathy's breathing altered, suddenly coming in short rasps. I knew instantly that this was a profound change. In a flash, I weighed whether to leave her bedside to ask the nurse to find Greg, but I knew instinctively that I couldn't leave at that moment. There was no time.

Thoughts bombarded me, even as the sense of time downshifted, each moment unfolding in slow motion. I rang the nursing bell and reminded myself to breathe, and to stay present with her and not to flee, either with my body or with my attention. I sensed an act of nature, a life-quake, occurring, and I stood almost outside myself for a split second, watching.

Dear God. She's going. It's happening. Right now.

Kathy was still. Her breathing, rale-y, raspy yet gentle, seemed not at all distressed, but in the next moments it began to change, her breaths coming more intermittently. I took her hand, staying near her face, which was soft, pink, peaceful, bent to the left towards me, as if listening.

I reached for some words to keep her company, to reassure her. "Remember, Honey, what we read about last night? Just go into the light. That light is you, too. Just relax into it.

You loved us all so well, you made such a beautiful life. We're so proud of you. We love you so much."

Then all went quiet. She took two short breaths, followed by two deep sighs.

I watched her, waiting for the next breath. But she was still.

She was gone.

I sat, the room vibrating with silence, and glanced at the clock: It was 11:11 am.

Responding to the bell, the nurse came in. All of this had transpired in a few short moments. She looked at me, and the look on my face told her everything she needed to know. She moved to the bed and placed her hand over Kathy's wrist, then nodded at me, confirming. She stayed a moment or two, gazing at Kathy. Then she whispered, "I'll go and get Greg."

Greg came rushing through the door. I left to give him privacy. When the rest of the family gathered, we circled the bed and held hands while Mom led us in praying the rosary. It's rote-ness and ancientness was an absolute comfort, something we could do together in that moment. I wondered whether on some level, even after her last breath, Kathy might still be able to hear, perhaps even "see" us.

The priest stopped in as we were finishing and assured my mother that he had come by earlier in the week and anointed Kathy with the Sacrament of the Sick. Someone brought in tea for my mom and me. We remained circled around the bed, with hands on Kathy's shoulder or her foot. I felt grateful again that my Mom and aunts had chosen not to shield us from death when we were young. It made this seem right somehow, not only to stay close during Kathy's long battle, but now, to not be skittish about staying with her for a while after she was gone.

The covering physician came by and told us how sorry he was, and how upset Dr. Lee had been that she had to leave. He told us how sad the staff were, which was amazing, given that this is the work they do every day. He hugged us, saying, "You've been a wonderful family, and we thank you because we learn from you. Whether you realize it or not, you made our job easier." He told us to stay as long as we needed to. Somewhere, somehow, a couple of phone calls were made. But, not wishing to break the spell in the room, we lingered, none of us quite ready to leave.

And then, life took over. Hunger set in and it was time to go. Time to pick her slippers up off the floor and watch as Kathy's nurses removed the last of the IVs and wheeled the pole out of the room. After we left, they would take care of her body, and the local funeral home in North Adams would transport her back home, as Greg and I had arranged. Now, all that was left for us to do was to pack up her few belongings: her robe, hairbrush, photos, and cards. The space itself was transforming; it was now a scene of aftermath.

We kissed her and left her in the sunny room in her pretty nightgown, with the covers drawn up around her shoulders as if she were tucked in for sleep. We closed the door and went out to the front desk, now cleared of staff for privacy except for her nurse, who hovered just out of the way, yet available. We stopped to thank her, then for the last time left the safe cocoon of the unit, where the staff had held us in their care. We made our way in a daze through the bustling halls of the hospital, and out into the blazing sun.

It felt like we were coming back from some sacred planet and having to rejoin the busy earthlings before we were ready. The drive home was vivid in its mundaneness. *Here I am stopped at a red light near Fenway Park, one of her favorite places on earth. And Kathy is gone.*

The sense of disorientation was profound. Part of me, part of my heart was left behind in that room. I had to will myself forward as we crossed town and headed home to carry on as best we could.

I want to be quiet for a long time.
— Anne Morrow Lindbergh

Aftermath

What took over next is what had seen us through: our togetherness. We drove home to Arlington in the mid-afternoon sun. Some tea was made. Some beers were opened. Mom went into mom mode and pulled out cans of tuna to make sandwiches. The house was quiet, voices hushed from fatigue and from crying. Family and friends were called. Then we gathered around the dining room table to eat and to divide a few simple next tasks among us. There was a measure of relief in taking on these next steps that move us forward at such a time. After sandwiches, Mom and I drove to the nearby photo store, with the picture we had chosen of Kathy to enlarge into a black-and-white print for the newspaper. Somehow, supper got made. The funeral home and rectory were contacted. Greg made the decision to stay the night with the boys and Mom, and to return to North Adams with them the next morning. Tony and I would follow the next day.

In the morning, some close friends came by, warm food in hand. It was both a relief and odd, after all those months, to not feel on high alert, and we felt grateful to be able to be ourselves, to weep or to stare, as they listened to the story of the past few days and helped answer the phone or the front door, as flowers were already arriving. We packed for North Adams in something of a trance, somehow making the routine decisions involved in leaving for a few days.

Kathy's wake took place, of all days, on Valentine's Day. Once again, we witnessed the deep, rich roots created when a life is lived out in tight community, as a parade of people Kathy had known from all the times and places of her life stood in line for hours to greet her family and say their good-byes. We wrapped her in a quilt that had been hand-made by Greg's mother, and the littlest cousins placed Valentine notes all around her.

The funeral day dawned cold but bright. The old church, which had seen generations of baptisms, marriages, and burials in our family, was filled and looked its finest with the February sunlight pouring through the old stained-glass windows and the altar decked with flowers. We could not help reflecting that we had occupied these same pews, and heard these same hymns and readings only months ago at my Dad's funeral. As then, the archetypal ritual was personalized by the roles taken on by close friends and family, as our cousins served as her pallbearers and Patrick and Liam brought forward the bread and wine to be consecrated for Communion. The organist was a boyhood friend and classmate of Patrick's.

At the Mass's end, Tony walked to the lectern with me and stood near as I offered the eulogy. I used a quote I had found from St. John Chrysostom: "She who we have loved and lose, is no longer where she was before. She is now wherever we are." I spoke about her gift for friendship, and her wit and bravery. I referenced her sports heroes, Carl Yastrzemski, Larry Bird, and said that any one of them would have been felled by what she had been through. She had gone through all of it for love, for more time with her husband

and sons, her family and friends. I said in closing, "From now on, whenever any of us is afraid of anything, just say her name inside your heart. And keep saying it 'til you've taken the plunge."

In the way of life pulling us forward, we returned from the graveside service at Southview Cemetery to a feast made by Kathy's neighbors, with plates of brownies and cake, trays of sandwiches, bowls of pasta and salads, and hugs everywhere you turned. As the afternoon went on, friends' children were brought to the reception, sweeping in with all their energy and life. Next thing I knew, someone was handing me a wriggling toddler and the hallway was filled with the sounds of 6-year-olds chasing one another, hair askew and shirttails flying. And suddenly, we were smiling and there was laughter again. I kept thinking that Kathy would have loved it.

It wasn't until the next day, when it was time to leave Greg and Liam to head back to Boston, that the really hard part began.

Southview

Beneath a tattered tarp flapping in the wind
encircled by the blue-gray hills
we sit.

Before us, newly turned earth, warm with steam,
and heaped with flowers

"We have come," intones the Deacon
"to bring our sister to rest."
Our sister. My sister. My chuckling, wise-
ass companion
Still now.

Mother of God
God our Mother
Do you hear us?
I am shrieking within, like David did in the psalms
like every Mother/sister/daughter/wife does,
imploring you,
like a six-year old, bolting through the door:
"Ma! (Are you there?) Ma! (I need you!) MA!
(Come quick!)"

God in the hillside
God in the clouds
God in the faces and hearts of those who
stand beside us

Kyrie Eleison
Lord, have mercy.
We are beyond words,
beyond prayer.
Only staring at those hills and at this pile of earth
and flowers
and recognizing we must go now.
If we believe in Your mercy,
all is well.
And we must leave
and feel the winter sun warm the backs
of our heads
as we walk away
to eat lunch and hold hands
and laugh at the babies
and squeeze old friends tight.

And we must marvel at the weather
(wasn't it kind to us today?)
and at the crowd
and at the feast made for us by many hands
eating slices of coffee cake,
and meatballs and multi-layered rainbow Jell-O

and we must begin
the steps that come after
the next steps
the moving on.
—February, 1999

She is Now Wherever We Are

Now and then, the thought shot through me like a news bulletin I was having trouble believing: *Kathy is gone.* My sister, my Irish twin, my best friend, was gone. The social worker from the hospital had mentioned a bereavement group, but, unsocial social worker that I had proven to be, I found I didn't really like the idea of talking about it with people. To my dismay, even when I shared the details with close friends, it quickly felt like "blah-blah-blah." Talking about it, at least at the beginning, felt as if it stripped it smaller somehow.

In quiet, it was vast. As soon as I began putting words to it, I wanted to stop and just go quiet again. Which, given my verbose nature, was an odd preference indeed. But there it was. And I was figuring this out in real time, so there were some awkward moments with friends when I started to pour it all forth, only to find myself suddenly wanting to pull back.

There were three things I had an insatiable need to do during the aftermath: to meditate, to read, and to keep my pen moving. As it had over the past two and a half years, the art studio and community continued to provide a refuge. These were my sustainment and my solace as I once again turned to my notebooks to try to assimilate what I was living.

We are snowed in after a major storm yesterday, the house brightened by the light reflecting off the snow drifts all around us. It's been two weeks now.

I am meditating in the mornings again, incorporating some things I've learned from my recent readings. It's only after Kathy's death that I've been able to read books on death and dying, suddenly hungry to hear about others' experiences. I'm trying to make some meaning of this event, which has rocked my world and left me feeling out of sync with everything around me. I find myself bewildered that while it feels as if we have survived an earthquake that has overturned life as we knew it, leaving a person, an essential person, missing, out there in the world things carry on as if nothing has happened. I feel perplexed and, truth be told, shocked. A part of me cries out, "How can this be? How can everything go on as if nothing has happened?" A cry that no doubt has been repeated ad infinitum down through the ages.

One of the books I liked best—somehow the language and form were such that I could easily take them in—was Christina Longaker's *Facing Death and Finding Hope*. A student of Sogyal Rinpoche, author of *The Tibetan Book of Living and Dying*, Longaker writes from a Buddhist perspective about losing her young husband to cancer and how that was the beginning of her own journey. She went on to become a pioneer in the hospice movement.

She gives very practical advice, but what was most helpful to my heart was a Buddhist practice she describes called Essential Phowa. I don't even know how it's pronounced, but it means sitting in meditation and calling up the image of your loved one being in the presence of Christ, or whatever holy being they may have had affection for, and meditating on that image, then seeing them merging with the being, and sending that image back out to them.

I found it tremendously comforting to do this practice every day. I felt lifted by it, soothed, and grateful to find something I could do that might have still helped her. And I could hope—for how do we know?—that somehow her spirit received the energy and intention of this way of praying for her, which I did seated on my trusty meditation cushion, with her photo and a candle lit on the bureau nearby.

I was preoccupied with remembering and sorting through the tumble of memories from the past months and especially, those last weeks. Night after night, Tony and I stayed up late, talking it all over. It seemed especially important to do this, and to write, while the details were still fresh. Remember this? Which night was that? Trying to fit the pieces together. I remembered doing this after Megan died so many years ago. Then, too, I felt compelled to review the whole ordeal again and again, needing to go back and revisit it before the memories, like dreams, slipped away. Every mundane moment now seemed so precious. I filled half a journal with memories from the last few weeks alone.

The remembrance cards that Greg's family created arrived in the mail, incorporating the quote from St. John Chrysostom I found to begin Kathy's eulogy, "She whom we love and lose, is now wherever we are," and the photo of Kathy laughing, from our wedding.

Kathy, 1997.

PSALM V
Benediction in Sunlight

Here is the same light that shone across her room,
all those last mornings while we sat
and prayed,
waiting for breathing to ease
that never eased.

This same light came streaming in then
through slatted hospital blinds
Across her face,
watching me,
it fell
across her cool, pale hands
and lit the room,
warming it,
when there was no other easing. And no words.

Blessed, blue-gold light that held us
in that still, late morning
when there was only the light
and the solemn quiet,
and her thin shoulders rising and falling.

It bathed the room in radiance,
glancing off the small red buttons on her nightgown,
and off the rings on the bed stand,
and off the photos of her sons.

It lit the long minutes
'til those last soft breaths,
just two wee sighs,
and then there was only the light,
and my heart beating,
and her silence

as she flew out to meet it.

A young nurse glides in
to take her wrist,
and give her soft assent:
yes. yes. she is gone. yes,
nodding into my eyes.
She leaves again
to summon the others
and prayers and goodbyes are whispered into the
light-drenched silence:
You go on now, sweetie. You go into the light.
We'll be okay. This is your day to shine.

It lit the long ride home
when there was nothing left to do,
and held us all that day
in a kind of embrace,
when nothing else could
touch or sanctify our sadness
but that light.

Like a gleaming trumpet
it shone out once again,
on the morning
when we buried her,
blazing in through stained-glass
and illuminating in jeweled color,
the ivory cloth
which covered her.
It danced up to meet the music
and wrapped about the words of scripture
as they pierced our hearts once more.

It lit the faces of all who came to circle her and
send her off,
the small-town church where she was baptized
and married,
filled with radiance
as she once more made her presence felt
in the passing dancing of the light.

There is a photo of her one August day,
and she is gay and dressed to dance,
the summer sun's caress
across her cheeks and shoulders
as she laughs and teases
through the lens.
It captures her, that moment,
in all her quick-tongued play,
having a laugh with the girls.

And that is how I see her now,
long days of illness melted, gone,
dwelling in the same presence
which now illuminates my morning room,
her spirit-laughter-heart as close beside as sunlight
on our bedquilt.

I recognize her there
and my heart smiles back in greeting.
—February 1999

March, 1999

Numb and Dumb

The phone was ringing. People were checking in, and I loved them for it, but I frequently found myself not knowing what to do with them yet. Perhaps it was time to reconnect, to pick up with what was going on out there in the world.

One evening in early March, Dr. Lee phoned to ask how we were all doing. She'd called Greg just before but didn't reach him, so she had left a message. She said she'd been very sad to be away that week, and that she'd thought of Kathy, and us, during her trip. She asked how it went. She wanted to hear. I told her it had been a "sweet" time with Kathy.

It seemed funny that I would say that, because it was hell. But there was also this sweetness. Every moment was so urgent and precious. There was a quality about her that was nearly childlike. No, that isn't totally right. It was more that she was so helpless and ill that it aroused in us the same sweetness of love and open-hearted tenderness that a new-born would. That same devotion and awe at witnessing this person so dear to us being completely herself, right up until she could no longer communicate. We sopped up every single second of connection with her, hanging on every moment, as if nothing else in the world mattered. For in fact, nothing else did. That's what I was trying to tell Dr. Lee.

To mark the day a month after she died, I meditated with a candle at the hour of 11:11 am, sending her calmness and light. I couldn't know, of course, whether she needed it or received it. For all I knew, *she* was sending *us* calmness and light from wherever she was. We travelled back to North Adams for the one-month anniversary Mass, and found there was something good and comforting about gathering again, this time with a smaller group of close ones than were present for the huge funeral.

After the Mass, we all went to dinner together, about fifteen of us gathered in the private back room of a small local restaurant. The décor was all vintage fifties, with black and white tile floors and a colorful though non-functioning jukebox. The room was next to the kitchen, so it was cozy-warm and filled with the savory smells of burgers and onions. The Saturday night buzz of conversation from the dining room next door was a comforting backdrop as our own conversation turned to memories of Kathy. Not for the first time, we reminisced about the night that Kathy and Greg met.

It was on New Year's Eve and, knowing Greg would be home from Norfolk Virginia on Navy leave and that both of them were dateless, I took a chance and fixed them up on a double date with my then-fiancé and me. Within the first ten minutes, Kathy and Greg began bantering in a way that reduced them both to peals of laughter and set the stage for a lifetime of banter to come.

At the table, Greg recounted how, on that cold winter night decades ago, he had helped Kathy on with her coat as we all bundled up and set out into the frigid evening. We were headed for a party at a local armory, transformed for the occasion with balloons and streamers, small lights and glittering favors, with a buffet and live band for dancing.

Lots of long-time friends would also be there.

"As we got to my car," Greg said, "I went to open the car door and Kathy took one look into the back seat. She saw the six-pack of beer I'd brought and shot me a look saying *Is that all you brought?!*" They had known each other for about half an hour. He had roared with laughter that night, and our table warmed with laughter at the memory.

My bookshelf reflected my search to understand what was happening. After reading Christina Longaker's book, I went looking for Sogyal Rinpoche's *The Tibetan Book of Living and Dying*. Despite the somewhat foreboding title, the text is quite accessible, almost conversational. Rinpoche talks about how in the West we are in danger of our busyness being all too effective in helping us avoid looking at death. But reflection upon it actually "helps us to refine our lives and not fill up with false studies and projects, while ignoring the 'Big Project.'" How we have all sorts of insurance, except "the Big Insurance" that meditation, contemplation, and spiritual practice can provide. It seemed so relevant, in light of what we had been living. He says that one of the most important things we can give to the dying is our presence. I thought we did this well for Kathy.

I was very fortunate to be granted time to recover. Exhausted on every level, I decided to extend the leave from my job for a few weeks, on the recommendation of my doctor. He was very kind as he completed the paperwork and encouraged me to not rush back into the thick of work.

He described a young doctor on his staff who had gotten burned out and told me, "You have a chance here to not let that happen to you, too." Underneath the fog of loss, I could touch gratitude.

The reality would hit at the oddest moments. While having my blood drawn at the doctor's office, I suddenly found myself flooded with emotion, flashing on how many times Kathy had done that, over and over again in all the various settings.

I kept in touch nightly with my mom and with Greg, reaching out by phone to put a hand on their shoulders at the end of the day. They were hanging on. Greg was very quiet, and Mom was having trouble sleeping—heartbroken, of course. And my girlfriends kept their hands on my shoulder as well, calling me often to check in. They were my sisters now.

The grief affected me physically: I was achy, preoccupied and weary, and just numb and dumb with missing her. There was a sense of disorientation, of repeated shock and readjustment to her missing-ness. There were mornings of waking up with a jolt of fresh pain, as I remembered as if learning it anew: *Oh right. Kathy is gone.* Yet, in my peripheral vision, I was aware of the need to move back into the tasks of my daily life.

I needed space and time for reading and remembering, meditating, and writing. I felt a craving—almost desperate—for silence, for sitting and staring, and for walking outdoors under the great canopy of sky, with the woods my new chapel. At the same time, I felt the pressure of so many things that needed our attention: the house, the mail, the bills, the finances, all the many earth-plane things that had been neglected during those last months. And we needed to navigate reconnecting with work, friends, and the outside world as well.

On the phone one night a friend asked if Kathy and I had any unfinished business. I thought about it and felt relieved to say, "No, thankfully, it burned pretty clean between us." How true that felt. How grateful I was for that.

Yet there were still waves of regret. Because while I lived and walked the journey beside her as best I could, we had rarely talked about it. Me! The big social worker! I could see that so clearly later. There were all kinds of feelings going on, which we communicated with our faces, with touch, with tenderness, and with dark humor. And there were certainly conversations about the decisions, the medical questions. But about the emotional journey? Not so much, until that day with Dr. Lee, when Kathy made the decision that she could go no further.

It was as if it was too big. Like staring into the sun, or approaching a mountain the size of Everest, any question of losing the battle seemed to strike me dumb. Despite the late-stage diagnosis from the outset, addressing the possibility of that loss remained unapproachable territory. The land of the unthinkable.

I wished I had been braver and raised those questions with her: *How are you really doing? Are you scared?* Such simple questions, which might have opened the door for her to be less alone with what she was facing. Yet my own terror of losing her made those conversations unbroachable, social worker or not.

I felt sure that she had talked more frankly about it with her caregivers: Dr. Lee and Dr. Spector, her nurses, and her Dana-Farber social worker. Maybe if I'd gone to those family groups the social worker kept inviting me to, I'd have had more courage. So, there was this kernel of regret to live with. And beside it, some mercy, a recognition that to some degree we were taking our cues from her, for whom the notion of leaving her family, her boys, had to bring the most searing pain. And a knowing that I did the best that I could—we all did—during a time when we often needed to set our own feelings aside to focus on the next step or emergency. It was easy to pass judgement in hindsight, having slept and re-covered some.

Regrets aside, I will always treasure that last night when I took my turn sleeping in her room. Even when we couldn't talk, we could sleep once more in that side-by-side compan-ionship we had shared as little girls in the bedroom with the awful wallpaper. I was exhausted, we all were, yet I hadn't wanted to waste the time we had left sleeping. I kept wak-ing during the night to sit up with her, holding her hand or talking or reading to her. It was, for all the heartbreak, one of the most alive moments of my life.

Then, like most families, after the funeral was over and the thank-you notes written, we were all lost for a while. Grief took hold and the sense of emptiness, sadness, and "why-bother?" was at times overwhelming. We struggled, each in our own ways, with the grayness that descended. The feeling for me was one of amputation. Someone who, since I was 13 months old, had been right at my elbow, was gone. It is a feeling that can still overtake me at family gatherings when for a nanosecond I think to turn and share some nugget or wisecrack, only to remember. Anyone who's been through it knows. Grief is raw and it is ugly. And it is physical—a heavy aching open-wound feeling, like the worst flu of the heart, so bad you think you may not make it through, but the bad news is, you know you will.

Tony and I continued to travel out to the Berkshires frequently, where we would circle up again and eat together, following Liam's high school activities like they were some North Star guiding us out of the desert. Patrick kept in touch from his campus an hour away. Games, band or school events, and family picnics became occasions to organize around, to continue to huddle together and to let more time pass.

Greg and Liam came to visit us in the spring, and I recorded it in my journal.

Journal: March 27, 1999

We have Greg and Liam with us this weekend. Patrick is at school, so it is just the two of them, their first visit here since Kathy's death. We wandered around Harvard Square in the evening, stopping at a place to eat where we had stopped many times with Kathy. We never gave it a thought until we were seated and then memories of the many times we had eaten here all together came swimming up for me. I found myself anxiously scanning their faces.

I finally blurted out "Is this okay?" and in sync they said, "Yes. It's fine." It was a good reminder, yet again, not to assume but simply to ask. I remembered that after I lost Megan, one of the most awful things was having people just ignore it. Better to be simple, but bring it up.

April, 1999

Going On

The burrowing down into the quiet went on. As the weeks passed, I continued to feel outside of time, aware of the world buzzing along beyond me, while I remained on slowed-down, turned-inward time. Holy time. Liminal time. Still making the journey back from the threshold of life and death.

Back here on the earth-plane, I still needed so much silence. Although I recognized the pull of events and people, I was still not ready to break the spell. The quiet, like being out in nature, was feeding something deep within me. Everything else felt too loud, too fast, jarring, like dishes clattering to the floor.

In the quiet, there was room still for tears, and room for God. Me and God staring at the hole in my heart. One side was bashed in, exploded like the building in the Oklahoma City bombing. And yet, miraculously, the other side was still perfectly good, still beating and doing its work. From that side, I could try to connect with the world out there, while the bashed-in side was in essential survival mode. I thought about all the people on the planet who carried on with bashed-in hearts, all day, every day, millions of them. There is not much place for wounded hearts in our speeded-up western culture. Our rituals are all very neat and time-limited and absent the loud wails that bashed-in hearts can easily give over to. I'd been blessed indeed to be able to take some extra time. Most people are expected to show up with their work faces on after three days. When you are among the walking wounded, you see clearly how insane this is.

As time went on, all kinds of things happened, and Kathy wasn't here: events and moments she would never have missed. She missed Liam's jazz concert at Chapin Hall at Williams, and the day he got his driver's license. She missed Roger Clemens going to the Yankees, though, we all agreed, she would have been happy to miss that one. Over and over, I tasted that feeling. Not mournful so much as still surreal.

Slowly, I began to reconnect with the web of friendship that had nourished Tony and me through the years. And, no doubt thanks to my Catholic roots, I continued to find comfort in ceremony to acknowledge and express the grief and loss. Longtime girlfriends, who I had not seen much during Kathy's illness yet considered soul sisters, took me out to the Sudbury River to do an afternoon ritual. They had called to say, "We want to do this with you, to make a river ritual for Kathy."

As we walked to the water's edge, I talked about how it had been towards the end. Then we built a small raft on a tree branch and I placed a photo of Kathy on it, along with a tiny statue of Kuan Yin, the goddess of compassion. We lit a votive candle and tossed flowers into the raft as I pushed it out into the churning river and let it go. Then, chilled by the dampness, we headed to a nearby Japanese restaurant for hot noodle soup and sake.

Again that spring, that other anniversary of the heart came around, of Megan's very brief but changing-every-thing-after life, 23 Marches ago.

Megan. I've always wondered what she would have looked like. Would she have had my (and my mom's and grandfather's) auburn hair? Small or tall? Brown eyes or blue? The memories and questions flooded in, intensified by the other recent heartbreak.

It was part of life's mystery that I felt like a different person from the young woman who bore that child. I remembered the small bedroom we had papered in yellow gingham with buttercup trim. The room itself had felt pregnant with hope, filled as it was with borrowed furniture and a hand-made cradle.

I had felt betrayed by my body back then, utterly helpless and confused and out of step with friends and family, who were having babies all around me. Years later, I was told by an intuitive healer that Megan "had never intended to come and stay." The sole purpose of her fleeting life, the woman told me, had been to "come across time, from a deep bond in another life, to make contact with you, to help you to give birth to a new life in this one."

And whatever I made of that message at the time, I could indeed look back and see a gift gleaming there in all the loss. From the vantage point of years later, I could recognize that we cannot know, as something is happening, what meaning it will hold for our lives. Things that look like walls can turn out to be windows that we fly through because we must, be-coming, on the way, a different person.

I could only know that all of the despair, confusion, and depression, and the feeling of being almost physically ejected from my previous life had led to this one. And from this realization emerged the sense of a soul-deep task being fulfilled. Heartbroken as I was, I felt a deep and completely unanticipated knowing that accompanying Kathy in whatever way I had was something my life had been meant for. And I could recognize and feel: *lucky me.*

How blessed to have followed the rock-strewn path that had gotten me here, able to walk these last three years with Kathy and her family, to have shared our lifelong journey as sisters, which ended in affection and peace. And blessed, yes, to be able to step forward now to help Greg and to take her boys even closer, as we all learned to walk on without her.

Strangely, I began daydreaming about going to Ireland. This felt more than a bit crazy at the time, but then again, crazy felt normal during the aftermath. Absent any identifiable reason, I'd begun to feel a fierce, almost biological pull to go, which was odd, since I'd never set foot in Ireland. Yet I found myself seized with a deep longing to go to the west of Ireland, specifically, to the coast. It was, as longings often are, a most inconvenient thing to acknowledge. I was just getting back to work. I had gone through all my savings. I had never been there and couldn't even articulate *why* I needed to go. Yet, go, I felt, I must. And, after talking it over a few times with Tony, go, it seemed, we would.

May, 1999

Limpets

Maureen and Tony burning documents at Galway Bay, Ireland, 1999.

In May, three months after Kathy's death, Tony and I left for Ireland, following the unexpected urge I'd felt to go "home." And indeed, it felt like home when we got there. Both of us experienced a similar reaction as we landed and walked through the airport in Dublin. It was an emotional connection that blindsided us, as we saw, in the faces and gestures of those walking past us, echoes of our cousins, aunts, uncles, and grandparents.

We rented a car and set out from Dublin along a meandering southern route across the country. Our first stop was in Kildare. There, at the holy well near the Cathedral of St.

Brigid, we strung Kathy's photo on a ribbon in a tree. Setting off for the west, we continued to find echoes of family everywhere. Further south in Wexford, we stopped at a welcoming spot for lunch. It was a lively place full of locals, including some school girls in uniforms circled into one of the corner booth tables, chattering and laughing together. A fire glowed, filling the room with the earthy smell of peat that we would find everywhere. A couple of old-timers hunched at the bar, hovering over their glasses, their animated conversation rising and falling in the lyrical music of Irish speech.

As we settled into our table, I noticed an elderly woman seated near the fireplace, bundled even in May into a frayed woolen sweater. I watched her thank her server, who set a steaming pot of tea down before her. When the woman proceeded to pour some of the contents into her saucer to cool it, then lift it to her lips to sip, my breath caught. I had witnessed my grandfather doing this again and again throughout my childhood, and I had written it off as some eccentricity of his. But here it was on display, I would learn, as a custom of the working class, brought from the old country.

We drove west through the center of the country, stopping along the way in places with names like Roscrea, Adare, Killarney, Kenmare, and Tralee. Our Irish friend Úna had handwritten an itinerary for us, including pubs to look up and names of their proprietors to be sure to say hello to. We made our way to a lodge in Ventry Bay on the Dingle Peninsula, where we stayed a few nights to sleep and walk and fight off colds. Then, one damp, chilly afternoon on the beach at Galway Bay, we took the piles of papers left at our house from Kathy's illness, the mounds of notes from VNA and Dana-Farber visits, sheets describing the various protocols and side effects of her meds, and papers from the endless hospital stays. Even this enormous pile was only half of the documents. The other half remained in North Adams in Greg's big black notebook. Having gotten his blessing, we made a fire amid the stones and burned them all.

Bending and kneeling on the damp, dark sand, we fed bundles of pages into the fire and watched the smoke rise as we listened to the beat of the surf against the rock-strewn beach. I had balked at tossing the paperwork into the trash. It felt emblematic of something too important, too epic, so burning them satisfied some sad, quiet need.

Staring into the flames, I thought about Kathy and how she would have loved to have seen this land. And I thought about the sets of sisters in my family, the strong Irish ones who taught us what we knew about how to be women. The sisters were the engines, the matriarchs of our family. As Kathy and I watched them cooking or shopping, hanging wallpaper or starching curtains, driving us to swimming lessons, or sitting with older relatives as they lay dying, we were absorbing some code or craft that would give shape and meaning to our lives. What we learned from the sisters who went before us would later see us through the rapids of cancer and to the very edge of life. Watching the flames leap, I said their names to myself: Mary, known as Mamie, and Margaret Callahan; Mary and Kate Smith; Catherine and Helen Smith; Alice and Margaret Dowling; Margaret, Alice, and Mildred Dowling; Carol and Diane Bleau. And now: Maureen and Kathleen Smith.

We lingered, watching the fire die out. Noticing all the seashells around us, I recalled that as a child Kathy had treasured her seashell collection, storing it carefully in a series of round oatmeal boxes. I tucked a few of the pyramid-shaped shells that I later learned were called "limpets" into my pockets, to take home as talismans.

Then, with the dampness rolling in, Tony doused the embers with water from the bay and reached for my hand. We made our way back into town to one of the colorful pubs that line Galway's streets and ordered warm food and hot tea. We quietly toasted and I noticed that something in my chest had released. The sadness was not gone, by any stretch. That was a deep presence that I would carry with me. But I was learning that it had a warm companion, gratitude. So much of what I had found in this journey seemed to not "make sense." But making room for the grief and listening to its seemingly crazy needs had helped me to visit this other place. A place that felt like grace.

I hadn't understood the urgency I'd felt to make the trip until we got there. But Ireland turned out to be medicine for our grief, with its untamed landscape and mercurial skies, mysterious and powerful enough to hold all that we came carrying. Like all who, having visited once, fall under the spell of Ireland, Tony and I finished our meal already talking about when we might come back.

Ten Years Later: September, 2009

Ireland, Again

Inis Mór, County Galway

Officiating at the wedding ceremony, Inis Mor, 2009
(Photo © Jenna Medina).

We are standing on a wet, grassy hillside before the twelfth-century ruin of St. Ciaran's Church on Inis Mór, largest of the Aran Islands off the western coast of Ireland. It is Patrick and Leah's wedding day.

It has been pouring incessant, monsoon-like rain in Ireland for the last two months. The locals we've met have offered us condolences for having traveled so far for our family wedding during this siege of rain.

"It's a shame," they've offered. "A pity, to come here for yer doins' during this rot!"

Our group of 55 friends and family are gathered in a pasture so saturated that the guests had to ford a small stream to make it to the wedding site. One of the emblematic photos of the day will show Liam in mid-air, arms flung out and face contorted with effort as he leaps over the stream in his best-man wedding coat.

My feet are sopping wet. And I am electric with happiness. For, at the hour of the wedding, after dark days and pelting rain—and after choosing an alternate site inside the hotel, so grim did this morning's prospects look for an outdoor wedding—the sun has broken through. The sky has opened for the first time in weeks, a dome of radiant blue, and as we begin the ceremony, our shoulders and hearts are warmed and, it feels, blessed by the sun.

Patrick and Leah had asked me and Leah's mom, Sue, to officiate at their wedding. We'd sat at my kitchen table in Boston three months earlier, eating pizza and working out the logistics as we planned the ceremony together.

I wrote the opening of the ceremony, the welcome, three nights ago at Devondell, our B&B back in Galway, attended to by our hostess, Berna. Full of questions, she drew out the story about the wedding, my sister, and our family, then proceeded to close off the glass doors of her living room to other guests, to light the mantle candles and the peat fire, and to fetch me a crystal glass of Bailey's on ice, saying, "There now, you do your writing. That's holy work ye have to do. No one will bother you, I'll see to't. And just ring me if you've need of anything."

And now we have come to the section of the ceremony that Patrick and Leah planned for honoring the loved ones who are no longer here. We alternate reading the names, starting with the grandparents. As each name is read, a family member steps forward to take a rose and crumple it into a glass bowl the bride and groom are holding. The petals will be tossed over the couple after the wedding vows.

We reach the moment when Sue reads Kathy's name.

And Liam steps forward to take the rose for his mother's memory and to stand before his brother and his bride, to place the petals in the bowl. I register two things. First, the hint of emotion, passing but moving, that flickers over Liam's face as he hears his mother's name and steps forward. And, a millisecond later, a gasp that ripples through the crowd as Tony pokes me in the ribs and points upward to the sky.

A rainbow has appeared above us. I am not making this up. Around the circle, people turn to look upward and then at one another with smiles of wonder. Greg and I lock eyes in disbelief. We all know that Ireland is a place of rainbows, but the timing of this one was extraordinary enough to raise the question of God—or at least Steven Spielberg—being involved.

The sun stays with us through the ceremony and long enough for a photo session of the bride and groom surrounded by the breathtaking landscape. So full is the beauty, fleeting sorrow, and overarching joy of the day that it feels as if a profound circle has come around. We have traveled back here, to the land where our, Kathy and my, mother-sister-aunt-grand-mother ancestors came from, for a family event of joyous magnitude, tinged with awareness of one who is missing.

Wedding portrait, Inis Mor, 2009 (Photo © Jenna Medina).

Before we leave the hillside, I slip behind the stone wall of the church ruins and bend to build a small cairn for her. Sometimes when I am watching the boys, as I pause to do in this moment, I imagine that their mother is able to somehow "borrow" my seeing, to look at them through my eyes. As if I'm watching them for her. Like their father, and with his loving care, they have grown into wonderful young men. Smart, quick, hilarious, and thoughtful.

"We did good, Sweetie." I whisper, setting an ivory rose against the stones that have kept vigil in this place for millennia. "We did real good."

I stand to look around. Inis Mór is a tiny isle in the north Atlantic, a place of raw beauty, lashed and worn by centuries of exposure to the elements. On its inclement days, the words barren and stark would easily fit. Now, with the sunlight pouring across the rolling green rock-strewn hillsides and reflecting in shimmering prisms off the blue sea all around, it is magnificent. A place of survival and transcendence, with a wildness that provides the perfect setting for this day.

My heart can still feel hollow, ragged with missing Kathy, surely. Yet then comes life and loved ones to pull me forward, savored more deeply for their precious presence, their gorgeous now.

Laughter comes rising next, over the stone wall from the wet-footed bridal party. It's time to drive back to the hotel. Time for the dancing to begin. And as I had found before in my life, unthinkable loss had come to include, to coexist somehow, with unimaginable grace.

Wingaersheek

Sea as blue
as blue on earth can get,
bouncing, cresting,
amusement-park August waves.

Foam speaking to us
cajoling us as it rises,
Foam singing and sparkling
and rinsing us clean.

The water womb-warm and gentle
beneath the lively surf
at this last hour of beach light.
The shoreline fringed with human dolphins
squealing and splashing
in the end-of-summer-sunset-sea.

Light of living gold,
like juicy August peaches
coating the beach-goers in luminous glaze,
Gilding them from behind,
haloed, all.

The tide washes in, painting the sand
in opal sparks
While the sun begins
its slow goodnight

behind the hillside houses.

Before me,
two maidens sway
in glittery bikinis,
arms wrapped round each other's perfect bodies,
whispering their stories close.

My day of silence ends in light
Sunset, this last Sunday of summer
when I have been on retreat
and Wingaersheek,
my monastery.

The sun replaced now
by a crown of clouds,
the sole adornment
in the great blue dome,
perched at the cusp of day
to wrap the last rays
in a passion of purple, rose, and gold.

A couple shoos their ten-year-olds into the surf
and stand at the rocks, knee deep,
wrapped in a single towel,
nuzzling.

In this moment,
the perfection of the day

and of the season,
revealed.

A moment of light so rich,
it is like a drop of nectar
dropped upon the heart
to warm the months to come.

A moment of light so welcoming
it feels like a friend
wrapping a warm arm 'round
and breathing the secret of happiness
into your ear.

A moment of light so exquisite,
it pains to watch it go.

On earth, it goes like this:
our most golden, precious moments must come to
letting go
and

more stunning than the sun
in its most dazzling farewell
Are these shining human hearts, which,
knowing this,

go on loving anyway.
—August, 2003

Afterword

I was fortunate during the writing of this book to be in touch with Kathy's former oncologist, Dr. Stephanie Lee, now on staff at the Fred Hutchinson Center in Seattle. I expressed my concern that since Kathy's very difficult transplant occurred 20 years ago, I didn't want to present her experience as representational of current practices. She wrote back, and I'm including her response here:

"The science and supportive care for hematopoietic cell transplantation continue to improve, as does the success rate, although we are still a long way from it being an adequately safe and effective therapy for all patients. Since Kathy's transplant, our understanding of HLA-matching and donor selection, conditioning regimens, supportive care (especially antibiotics and antifungal treatments), and monitoring for complication (especially for viruses) has increased substantially. We are able to use less-intensive regimens to prepare people's bodies to accept donor cells, so they are not as beat up by the procedure before the transplant even has a chance to work. The field of autologous immunotherapy (using both cells and medications) is growing rapidly, potentially offering the advantages of a new, revitalized immune system without the risks of putting a donor's immune system into a patient. While transplant technology is getting better, we still have many people who get graft-versus-host disease and/or relapse after transplant. Organ damage is still a concern, and lung complications still cause many deaths.

What has not changed is the vulnerability, bravery, and dignity of the patients who embark on this journey, for whom the risks are outweighed by a chance for more time and life with beloved friends and family."

—Dr. Stephanie Lee, MD MPH
Professor at Fred Hutchinson Cancer Research Center and the University of Washington

Acknowledgements & Gratitudes

In a book about love, it can be no surprise that it was loved into being by the attention and encouragement of many people over such an expanse of time.

Indeed, as I sit finishing, my heart travels all the way back to the Sisters of St. Joseph and to Walter Gaffney, our high school principal, for the care they took to see and to nourish the goodness in us. They planted seeds of caring-that-turns-into-action that I feel, still.

To the community of North Adams and its good people who were so there for my sister and her family before, during, and after.

To my Mom & Dad, my extended family, and especially to the aunties. From them we learned by heart what caring for others meant.

To Kate Ransohoff, who I met at midlife, and to the incredible, very human, very magical community she founded decades ago. To all of my fellow Turtle Studio buddies who have listened, encouraged, read pages, danced, carved, played, painted, and sculpted beside me, keeping me company in Making and keeping my heart lifted and inspired. I am ever grateful for your love and friendship and for the Hum we make together.

To Kathleen Spivack, Boston writing coach & doula for this book. She drew the story out of me after I'd brought her a completely different project, then sat with me in her kitchen poring over draft after draft, bringing her years of experience and hawk eye to the manuscript.

To my healer women, Heather Chatfield and A. Hing-Lan Lo, acupuncturists who gently helped care for my physical well-being as I wrote.

To Ellen Weiden, Paula D'Arcy, Evelyn Gladu, and Andrea Winslow for listening that turned into healing in the deep places.

To Kathy's dedicated caregivers: Toni Dubeau, RN, MSN, NP; Stephanie J. Lee, MD, MPH; and Jesse Spector, MD. You don't find better humans than these—we were blessed to have them as our medical team. I was able to find each of them after twenty years, and they each graciously read and commented on relevant aspects of this book.

Very particularly, to my writing group of nearly twenty years: Carol Gray, Ellie Coolidge-Behrstock, Ellen Morrison, and Elisabeth Gaines, who practically have this work memorized. For all the coffee & meals, silence & laughter, wine & chocolate, tears & encouraging pushes, from Taos to Ashfield, from Maine to Medford.

To my other writing buddy, Irene Yeh, MD, M.P.H., for your careful reading and comments. Our Brookline 'Two Busy Chicks' mornings and chats over coffee laid the tracks for me to finish.

To Úna Barrett for so cheerfully being my editor of all things Irish.

To Patricia Crotty of Gray Dove Press for her clarity, her warm encouragement, and the fine editing she brought to this project. To Harvey Shepard, whose labor of love created the beautiful cover and total design of the book.

To all my readers for "holding" and thus helping birth this story: Emily Jeep-Klingaman, Joan Fitzgerald, Susan Maxwell, Susan Jones, Sue Cross, Tempe Goodhue, Nancy Goodman, Suzanne McLeod, Madeline Waife, Kate Flannery Silc, Sally Plone, and Jill Schlanger.

To my meditation group of over three decades: Janice Perates, Peter Mullen, and our departed but nonetheless beloved Christine Mullen. And to Janice for being the medicine woman who made my healing circle happen.

To libraries, in particular the North Adams Public Library, where I learned to love books, and grew up doing homework in the turquoise children's room.

To Fr. John Unni and the community of St. Cecilia's, Boston, for reviving my belief that faith shines best in acts of mercy, in music, and in wicked good humor.

To Robin, Leah, Dana, Arley, Jelissa & Zi for the love they bring daily to Kathy's "boys."

To Brenna Kathleen Smith, soon to be M.P.H., who carries her auntie's name and, by who she is, does her namesake proud.

To Carla and Drew, Jordan and Yan, Annika & Asa, Leo & Nina, for so much joy, and for their patience through all the detours and preoccupations of finishing this book.

To The Beatles. Seriously. Those pied pipers of the world were early teachers that, come what may in life: war, childhood illness, even the deaths of mothers, you can choose to reach for, make, and spread Joy. Special wink to Ringo.

Bibliography

Alexander, Elizabeth. *The Light of the World: A Memoir*. Grand Central Publishing, 2015.

Anthony, Carol K. *A Guide to the I Ching, Third Edition*. Anthony Publishing Company, 1988.

Baldwin, Christina. *Life's Companion: Journal Writing as a Spiritual Quest*. Bantam Books, 1991.

Berg, Elizabeth. *Escaping into the Open: The Art of Writing True*. Perennial Books, 2000.

Braden, Barclay, Ph.D. *Faith at Hand: Finding My Way to Depth Journaling*. Kindle ed., 2018.

Caldwell, Gail. *Let's Take the Long Way Home: A Memoir of Friendship*. Random House, 2011.

Cameron, Julia. *The Artist's Way*. Tarcher, 1992.

Capacchione, Lucia, Ph.D., A.T.R, R.E.A.T. *The Power of Your Other Hand: Unlock Creativity and Inner Wisdom Through the Right Side of Your Brain*. Weiser Publishing, 2000.

Chödrön, Pema. *When Things Fall Apart: Heart Advice for Difficult Times*. Shambhala Publications, 1996.

Cody Pat. *DES Voices: From Anger to Action*. DES Action Publications, 2008.

D'Arcy, Paula. *Winter of the Heart: Finding Your Way Through the Mystery of Grief*. Ave Maria Press, 2018.

Dass, Ram, and Mirabai Bush. *Walking Each Other Home: Conversations on Loving and Dying*. Sounds True, 2018.

Gawande, Atul. *Being Mortal*. Metropolitan Books, Henry Holt & Company, 2014.

Gilbert, Elizabeth. *Big Magic: Creative Living Beyond Fear*. Riverhead Books, 2016.

Groopman, Jerome, MD. "A Healing Hell." *The New Yorker*, October 19, 1998.

Groopman, Jerome, MD., and Pamela Hartzband, MD. *Your Medical Mind*. Penguin Press, 2011.

Killilea, Marie. *Karen*. Prentice Hall, 1952.

Lamott, Anne. *Bird by Bird: Some Instructions on Writing and Life*. Anchor Books, 1995.

Leary, Lani, PhD. *No One Has to Die Alone: Preparing for a Meaningful Death*. Atria Paperbacks, Simon & Schuster, 2012.

Levine, Stephen. *Healing into Life and Death*. Anchor Press, 1989.

Levine, Stephen. *A Year to Live: How to Live this Next Year as if It Were Your Last*. Bell Tower, 1998.

Levine, Steven, and Ondrea Levine. *Who Dies? An Investigation of Conscious Living and Conscious Dying*. Anchor Press, 1989.

Lindbergh, Anne Morrow. *War Within and Without*. Harcourt Brace Jovanovich, 1980.

Longaker, Christine. *Facing Death and Finding Hope: A Guide to the Emotional and Spiritual Care of the Dying*. Main Street Books, 1998.

Middlebrook, Christina. *Seeing the Crab, A Memoir of Dying*. Basic Books, 1999.

National Cancer Center. *Bone Marrow Transplantation Research Report #92-1178*. US Dept. of Health and Human Services, April, 1991.

Okun, Barbara, Ph.D. and Joseph Nowinksi, Ph.D. *Saying Goodbye: A Guide to Coping with a Loved One's Terminal*

Illness. Harvard Health Publications, 2011.

O'Rourke, Megan. *The Long Goodbye: A Memoir*. Riverhead, 2012.

Pattee, Rowena. *Moving with Change, A Woman's Re-Integration of the I Ching*. Arkana Paperbacks, 1986.

Ransohoff, Kate. *Elijah's Palace*. KRQ Publishing, 2008.

Remen, Rachel Naomi, MD. *Kitchen Table Wisdom: Stories that Heal*. Riverhead Books, 1996.

Rinpoche, Sogyal. *Tibetan Book of Living and Dying*. Harper, 1992.

Roberts, Elizabeth, and Elias Amidon, Eds. *Life Prayers from Around the World: 365 Prayers, Blessings, and Affirmations to Celebrate the Human Journey*. Harper, 1996.

Rosenberg, Larry. *Living in the Light of Death: On the Art of Being Truly Alive*. Shambhala Publications, 2000.

Sarton, May. *Plant Dreaming Deep*. W.W. Norton & Company, New York, 1968.

Wilber, Ken. *Grace and Grit: Spirituality and Healing in the Life and Death of Treya Killam Wilber*. Shambhala Publications, 2001.

Willis, Claire B., LICSW. *Lasting Words: A Guide to Finding Meaning Toward the Close of Life*. Green Writers Press, 2013.

For musical accompaniment: Dana Cunningham's "Dancing at the Gate," "Above the Field," "Live at Stone Mountain Arts Center," and "The Color of Light." (Available at www.danacunningham.com.)

Maureen & Kathy, 1997.

Made in USA - Kendallville, IN
82183_9781953253002
11.10.2021 1209